PRAISE FOR THE
UNCOMMON JUNIOR HIGH GROUP STUDIES

The *Uncommon* Junior High curriculum will help God's Word to become real for your students.

Larry Acosta
Founder of the Hispanic Ministry Center, Urban Youth Workers Institute

The best junior high/middle school curriculum to come out in years.

Jim Burns, Ph.D.
President of HomeWord (www.homeword.com)

A rich resource that makes genuine connections with middle school students and the culture in which they live.

Mark W. Cannister
Professor of Christian Ministries, Gordon College, Wenham, Massachusetts

A landmark resource for years to come.

Chapman R. Clark, Ph.D.
Professor of Youth, Family and Culture, Fuller Theological Seminary

Great biblical material, creative interaction and *user friendly*! What more could you ask for? I highly recommend it!

Ken Davis
Author and Speaker (www.kendavis.com)

A fresh tool . . . geared to make a lasting impact.

Paul Fleischmann
President and Co-founder of the National Network of Youth Ministries

The *Uncommon* Junior High curriculum capitalizes both GOD and TRUTH.

Monty L. Hipp
President, The C4 Group (www.c4group.nonprofitsites.com)

The *Uncommon* Junior High curriculum is truly cross-cultural.

Walt Mueller
Founder and President, Center for Parent/Youth Understanding (www.cpyu.org)

The creators and writers of this curriculum know and love young teens, and that's what sets good junior high curriculum apart from the mediocre stuff!

Mark Oestreicher
Author, Speaker and Consultant (www.markoestreicher.com)

This is serious curriculum for junior-highers! Not only does it take the great themes of the Christian faith seriously, but it takes junior-highers seriously as well.

Wayne Rice
Founder and Director, Understanding Your Teenager (www.waynerice.com)

The *Uncommon* Junior High curriculum fleshes out two absolute essentials for great curriculum: biblical depth and active learning.

Duffy Robbins
Professor of Youth Ministry, Eastern University, St. Davids, Pennsylvania

It's about time that curriculum took junior-highers and youth workers seriously.

Rich Van Pelt
President of Alongside Consulting, Denver, Colorado

The *Uncommon* Junior High curriculum will help leaders bring excellence to every lesson while enjoying the benefit of a simplified preparation time.

Lynn Ziegenfuss
Mentoring Project Director, National Network of Youth Ministries

UNCOMMON
be extraordinary.

LISTENING TO GOD

KARA POWELL
General Editor

Published by Gospel Light
Ventura, California, U.S.A.
www.gospellight.com
Printed in the U.S.A.

Contributing writers: Kara Powell, PhD, Natalie Chenault and Siv Ricketts.

Library of Congress Cataloging-in-Publication Data
Uncommon jr. high group study : listening to God / Kara Powell, general editor.
p. cm.
Includes bibliographical references and index.
ISBN 978-0-8307-6136-4 (trade paper : alk. paper)
1. Obedience—Religious aspects—Christianity—Study and teaching. 2. Listening—
Religious aspects—Christianity—Study and teaching. 3. Spirituality—Study and teaching.
4. Church work with teenagers. 5. Church group work. 6. Teenagers—Religious life—
Study and teaching. I. Powell, Kara Eckmann, 1970- II. Title: Uncommon junior
high group study. III. Title: Listening to God.
BV4647.O2U53 2011
268'.432—dc23
2011042705

Rights for publishing this book outside the U.S.A. or in non-English languages are
administered by Gospel Light Worldwide, an international not-for-profit ministry.
For additional information, please visit www.glww.org, email info@glww.org, or write
to Gospel Light Worldwide, 1957 Eastman Avenue, Ventura, CA 93003, U.S.A.

To order copies of this book and other Gospel Light products in bulk quantities,
please contact us at 1-800-446-7735.

Contents

How to Use the Uncommon Junior High Group Studies

Each *Uncommon* junior high group study contains 12 sessions, which are divided into 2 stand-alone units of 6 sessions each. You may choose to teach all 12 sessions consecutively, or to use just one unit, or to present each session separately. You know your group, so do what works best for you and your students.

This is your leader's guidebook for teaching your group. Electronic files (in PDF format) for each session's student handouts are available online at **www.gospellight.com/uncommon/jh_listening_to_God.zip.** The handouts include the "Reflect" section of each study, formatted for easy printing, in addition to any student worksheets for the session. You may print as many copies as you need for your group.

Each individual session begins with a brief overview of the "big idea" of the lesson, the aims of the session, the primary Bible verse and additional verses that tie in to the topic being discussed. Each of the 12 sessions is geared to be 45 to 90 minutes in length and is comprised of two options that you can choose from, based on the type of group that you have. Option 1 tends to be a more active learning experience, while Option 2 tends to be a more discussion-oriented exercise.

The sections in each session are as follows:

Starter
Young people will stay in your youth group longer if they feel comfortable and make friends. This first section helps students get to know each other better and focus on the theme of the lesson in a fun and engaging way.

Message
The Message section enables students to look up to God by relating the words of Scripture to the session topic.

Dig

Unfortunately, many young people are biblically illiterate. In this section, students look inward and discover how God's Word connects with their own world.

Apply

Young people need the opportunity to think through the issues at hand. The apply section leads students out into their world with specific challenges to apply at school, at home and with their friends.

Reflect

This concluding section of the study allows students to reflect on the material presented in the session. You can print these pages from the PDF found at **www.gospellight.com/uncommon/jh_listening_to_God.zip** and give them to your students as a handout for them to work on throughout the week.

Want More Options?

An additional option for each section, along with accompanying worksheets, is available in PDF format at **www.gospellight.com/uncommon/ jh_listening_to_God.zip**.

UNIT I

Seeking God's Voice

"Practical theology."

These two words leapt from the seminary brochure I was reading.

"Practical theology."

That's it, I thought. *That's the concentration I want for my doctoral studies.*

Some may think of practical theology as a contradiction in terms. My response is that it's actually redundant. At its core, the field of practical theology is based on the belief that what we think about God (the theology part) influences how we act (the practical part). It's impossible to divorce our beliefs about God from our actions. The way we view other people, our work, our possessions and even things as seemingly mundane as eating and driving are all reflections of who we believe God is and who we believe He wants us to be.

The same is true of the topic of this study. I know few believers who feel satisfied with their dedication and ability to hear God's voice (including myself). I'd like to suggest that any difficulty we have with hearing God's voice ultimately resides in some misperception we have about God.

Maybe we think *God is too busy to talk with us.* After all, He's got seven billion folks on the planet to keep an eye on. How can He have the energy to focus on little ol' you or me? Or perhaps we believe *God doesn't speak anymore.* Times change, communication methods change, and it's logical that somehow God's voice has been muted a bit. Given that He doesn't have an email address, He's a bit out of the loop.

Or maybe it's because deep down we believe *God doesn't speak to someone like us.* Sure, in biblical times He spoke to folks like Isaiah, Jeremiah and Paul, but they were a different kind of people in a different kind of time. I know people today who have heard from Him, either through an audible voice, or more commonly from an impression they knew was divine, but there must be something about those kinds of people that is special and unique. When they were passing out bionic ears, we must have been in the wrong line.

If we take even a few seconds to analyze these perceptions about God, we realize how foolish they are. God can't be "too busy," as He transcends our sense of time and schedule. Because His nature is constant, He can't have gone mute all of a sudden. And there doesn't seem to be a unique profile of the kind of person to whom God speaks. God seems to have broken through to all sorts of people regardless of their background and personality.

That's why I think it's something even deeper. What is it ultimately that keeps us from hearing from God? We can blame it on our schedule, but if the President of the United States wanted to say something to us every morning, we would certainly make time for it, because we value that person's input and position. So maybe the real question is, *How much do we really value God?* If we really believe that we need God and are helpless without Him, then we would go running to Him for guidance and strength, just as a toddler runs to his or her parents. Maybe we've lost some of that childlike faith and reliance. Maybe we've become more like sullen teenagers who greet our heavenly Father with a "hey, how's it going?" kind of salutation, while our attention quickly returns to the TV show we're watching instead of actually waiting for His answer.

We've planned this book with one major hope: that it will remind you and your students of *why* you need to hear God and *how* you can be more receptive to His voice. But ultimately, even the most creative game or best case study will not produce a change in behavior without a change in you and your students' basic beliefs. So we're back to where we started: our practical theology.

Is God really the source of strength for your life that you claim Him to be? Are you really convinced that you need—really need—God to guide you? Let me leave you with one last question: If someone was to peer into your life and answer those two questions by looking at the time you set aside to listen to God, what kinds of answers would that person come up with? Hmmm . . .

Kara Powell
Executive Director of the Fuller Youth Institute
Assistant Professor of Youth, Family and Culture
Fuller Theological Seminary

SEEKING GOD'S VOICE IN HIS WORD

THE BIG IDEA

As we seek and obey what God has told us in His Word, we will experience greater long-term benefits.

SESSION AIMS

In this session, you will guide students to (1) understand that obeying God's Word leads to both tangible and intangible blessings; (2) feel motivated to make hard choices now, knowing that they will experience greater long-term benefits later; and (3) act by choosing at least one of the Ten Commandments they need to obey in a greater way this week.

THE BIGGEST VERSE

"Be strong and very courageous. Be careful to obey all the law my servant Moses gave you; do not turn from it to the right or to the left, that you may be successful wherever you go" (Joshua 1:7).

OTHER IMPORTANT VERSES

Exodus 20:1-17; Joshua 1:1-9; 3:17; Jeremiah 29:13; Romans 6:1-2; Ephesians 6:2-3; James 1:23-24

Note: Additional options and worksheets in 8$^1/_2$" x 11" format for this session are available for download at **www.gospellight.com/uncommon/jh_listening_to_God.zip**.

STARTER

Option 1: Hit the Mute Button. For this option, you will need a way to re-cord or download TV shows and a way to play them for your group. You will also need a few adult volunteers, so if you don't have any handy, make sure to invite a few parents who can really ham it up to join you for this lesson.

Ahead of time, record or download at least two of your students' favorite TV shows. If you don't know what those favorite shows are, just ask them! They're sure to have lots of opinions. Watch the shows ahead of time to find a two- to three-minute clip that is full of dialogue and action, but where it's tough to tell without listening to the actors' lines what is actually happening (for instance, what they're mad about, what they're excited about, and so forth). Also ahead of time, meet with a few volunteers to let them know they will be acting out some TV scenes, but that they will not know what is actu-ally happening in these scenes. Encourage them to be as outlandish as possi-ble, even if their lines hardly make sense (in fact, the less they make sense, the better!). Make sure that they haven't seen the shows already and that they are pretty good at spontaneously acting things out.

Greet your students when they arrive and ask them to list some of their favorite TV shows. After they have yelled out their favorites, explain how you have taped some of last week's episodes of a few popular shows. However, they are going to be watching these scenes with the sound off, and they need to figure out what is going on. Play the first TV show clip with the volume muted or turned all the way down, making sure that students who have seen the show already don't yell out what is taking place.

Call up the adult volunteers you chose before the meeting. Ask the volun-teers to act out what they just saw to the best of their abilities. Tell them that because they didn't hear anything, they will have to make up the actors' lines, motivations and any relevant background information. They can't talk to each other to come up with a plot ahead of time, so they will just have to wing it.

After the adult volunteers are finished, ask if any of the students have seen the actual episode of the TV show. Choose a few of these students to come forward and act out what actually happened in the scene. If you have time, repeat this with one or two scenes from other TV shows. When you're done, ask the group what they think the difference was between what the adult vol-unteers acted out and what the students acted out. (The answer should be that the adults had no idea what was going on, as they couldn't hear the show, but the students were familiar with the scenes so they could act out the lines and the scenes more accurately.)

Explain to the group members that we will be starting a new series on seeking God's voice. Many people think it is difficult to hear God's voice or that He doesn't speak at all to people today. However, God has already spoken to us in His Word, and we don't have to wonder what He is saying to us as if we were watching Him on TV with the mute button on. He's already given us tons of instructions and great stories about Himself. As we will see today, the more we obey what He's already told us, the better the long-term benefits will be.

Option 2: Guessing Game. For this option, you will need copies of the "Guessing Game" cards (found on the next page). Greet students and have them get into groups of 8 to 10 students each. Have each group pick one volunteer, and then ask the volunteers to leave the room. Distribute one "Guessing Game" card to each group, and have each group read the instruction on the card. Everyone in that group will answer his or her volunteer's questions according to what the card says.

Have the volunteers return to the room and join their groups. Explain to the volunteers that they need to ask questions of the group members. By listening to the answers, they will be able to figure out what the group is doing. Some examples of questions would be, "Liz, what is your favorite color?" or "Jason, if you could have any car, what would you have?"

When all volunteers have guessed what their group is doing, you can repeat this game with a new group of volunteers. After playing this game a few times, ask the volunteers the following questions:

- How did it make you feel when you had to guess what your other group members were doing but had no idea what was going on?
- How would it make you feel if all of your conversations with others were this hard?
- How would it make you feel if this were the only way you had to communicate with God—by always guessing what He was trying to say?

Explain to the group that we don't have to guess what God is trying to say to us. Today, you will be starting a series on how we can seek God's voice and hear what He has to say to us. During today's lesson, they will learn that God has already communicated to us through His Word, and that the more we follow and obey what He has already told us to do, the better the long-term benefits will be.

Guessing Game

Answer as if you were the person sitting on your left.

Answer as if you were the person sitting on your right.

If any part of your body is crossed (your legs are crossed, your arms are crossed in front of you), you should lie.

If you're a boy, answer like you're 4 years younger.

If you're a girl, answer like you're 10 years older.

Only use your left hand when you're talking, but use it a lot.

When you answer, make sure you touch some part of your face.

Answer as if you were the person asking you the question.

MESSAGE

Option 1: Clues. For this option, you will need a Bible, a prize, adult volunteers and a variety of rooms. Your adult volunteers will be hiding in the rooms, so ahead of time, find out where they plan to conceal themselves so you can give your students hints as to where they are located. You might want to try to darken all of the rooms to make the game a bit harder. Also, make sure you have some way of letting everyone know the game is over (a bullhorn, a whistle, or even a loud yell) so that adults don't stay in hiding and miss the rest of the lesson. (*Note*: If you don't have enough adults or access to a variety of rooms, you can use your own meeting room and hide a few stuffed animals or dollar bills instead. Change the directions of the game to fit your situation.)

Have the adult volunteers leave the room. Divide the students into groups of five to seven people. Explain that they will be playing a game where they will need to search as a team for the adult volunteers who are hidden throughout the house/building/church campus (whatever fits your setting). If they find one of the adults, they have to carry—yes, *carry*—him or her back to the meeting room. (Make sure to advise them to be careful when they are doing this so you don't have any injuries.) When they achieve this task, you will give that team 1,000 points. They can then run back out to try to find another adult and carry him or her to the meeting room as well. The winning team gets a prize.

Begin the game. When a team arrives with an adult volunteer, award them their points and then whisper the location of where they can find the next hidden adult. In other words, tell them where to go to find an adult. They will not know this ahead of time.

End the game by using your preferred method of noise after 10 to 15 minutes, or when all of the adults have been found. Bring your students back together and ask what they think the difference was between the first time they ran out to find an adult and the second, third and fourth times. (The answer should be that you gave them hints on the second, third and fourth times.)

Youth Leader Tip

Always try to build relationships with parents and make them your allies. Invite them to observe the group and participate in some meetings. After all, they are more influential in your students' lives than you are!

State that in the same way, it is easier to know what we are supposed to do in life when we are given the answers. Fortunately for us, we have been given all kinds of clues and answers about what we are supposed to do. We just have to know what they are and then follow them.

Explain that in the Bible a man named Joshua learned this lesson. When Moses died, God chose Joshua to lead the Israelites. Joshua had been second in command, but now he was the head honcho. He had some pretty big shoes to fill. However, as we'll see, God had a special plan for Joshua. He gave Joshua three major jobs: (1) conquer the land that He had promised to give the Israelites (Joshua 1–12); (2) distribute the land among the people (Joshua 13–19); and (3) obey the law (Joshua 20–24).

Read Joshua 1:1-9 aloud, placing special emphasis on verses 6-9. When you are finished, ask the group the following questions:

- What did God mean when He told the Israelites to obey "all the law my servant Moses gave you"? (*God was referring to the Ten Commandments and other laws that He had given to Moses and the priests. These laws already had been written down for them. This would have made it easier for the Israelites to remember and to apply them to their lives.*)

- What does the Bible say would happen to Joshua if he obeyed the laws that God had already given to Moses? (*Things would go well with him.*)

- How is this like the adult scavenger hunt we just played? (*When we had hints about where to go, things went much better.*)

- What laws has God given us to obey? (*He has given us many more than just the Ten Commandments. We are blessed to have both the Old and New Testaments in the Bible that tell us exactly what God wants us to do.*)

- But isn't the whole Bible a lot to obey? (*Yes it is, but once you understand the basic principles of who God is and how Jesus lived here on earth, it gets easier to figure out what God wants you to do.*)[1]

If you have time, you might want to flip ahead in Joshua and summarize some of the things that happened when Joshua and the Israelites obeyed God. For example, in Joshua 3:1-17, after 40 long years of wandering, they were able to cross the Jordan River and enter the Promised Land. The Jordan River was no little stream—it was a real river, and certain parts of it were very wide and hard to cross. In Joshua 3:17, the priests carried the Ark of the Covenant into the middle of the river, and a path opened up.

Encourage the group to begin to read God's Word daily to discover what an awesome future God has for them. The same promise that God made to Joshua in 1:7 is also true for them. They can know for certain that when they seek out God's voice in His Word and follow what He says, He will bless them and be with them.

Option 2: Fortune Cookies. For this option, you will need a Bible, fortune cookies, and an adult volunteer who will share childhood pictures of himself or herself. Ahead of time, meet with the adult volunteer. Have this person choose pictures of himself or herself that represent a glimpse of God's blessings (such as family relationships, chances to go to school, good friendships). The volunteer should be ready to share the pictures as the meeting begins.

Begin by asking someone to share a time when he or she had to follow a presentation by someone who really did a great job. How did it make him or her feel? Chances are it made the person feel anxious, because following a great presentation sets a high standard that he or she would want to meet. Well, the same was true of a man in the Bible named Joshua. Joshua was the right-hand man of Moses, a great leader whom God had used to take the Israelites out of slavery in Egypt. God had been very close to Moses, and he had used him to do some miraculous things. When Moses died, God chose Joshua to be his successor—which were some pretty big shoes to fill. God also gave Joshua three very big goals to meet: (1) conquer all of the people living in Canaan, which God had promised to give to His people (Joshua 1–12); (2) distribute the land among the people (Joshua 13–19); and (3) instill in the people the need to obey the law (Joshua 20–24).

Read Joshua 1:1-9, and explain that when Joshua did what God told him to do, things went well for him. In the same way, when we do the things that God tells us to do in His Word, things will go better—*much* better—for us. However, obeying God will only be possible if we trust Him. If we don't think God will come through for us when we need Him, we probably won't follow what He says. Fortunately, this passage shows us that God has a history of keeping His promises.

At this point, ask your volunteer adult to share his or her pictures with the group and how those pictures are symbols of God's faithfulness. When the volunteer is finished, explain to the group how most of us probably have pictures of ourselves that show how God blessed us when we were growing up. The same is true with Joshua. As he followed Moses around, he would have witnessed firsthand the ways that God rescued the people again and again. So when God told him, "As I was with Moses, so I will be with you; I will never leave you nor forsake you" (verse 5), it would have really hit home. Based on this past history, Joshua could trust God when He revealed what would happen in the future: He would be with Joshua and help him lead the people into the Promised Land.

Distribute the fortune cookies and watch as your students dig into them and eagerly read their fortunes. Ask students to think about whether or not they open their Bibles and read it to find out about their futures in the same way they opened their fortune cookies. Encourage them to begin to read God's Word daily to discover what an awesome future God has for them. Conclude by stating that the same promise God made to Joshua is true for them. They can know that when they seek out God's voice through the Bible, God will bring blessings into their lives.

DIG

Option 1: The Ultimate Price. For this option, you will need a whiteboard and a whiteboard marker. Ahead of time, make three columns on the whiteboard.

Ask the group to think of ways that people their age often disobey what God has told them to do in the Bible. As the group members give you their answers, write their ideas in the first of the three columns on the whiteboard. You and your students will probably come up with quite a list, ranging from cheating and swearing to vandalism to premarital sex. Next, go on to column two. In this column, have the group members come up with at least one benefit for each activity in column one. For example, when they cheat, they might get better grades; when they swear, they are more like the other students at school; when they vandalize property, they look cool; when they are willing to have sex, they get more attention from the opposite sex.

In the third column, again go through each of the activities in column one, but this time have the group members come up with negative consequences they might experience from doing these things. For example, when they cheat, they don't learn; when they swear, they develop a habit that becomes hard to stop; when they vandalize, they destroy things that are valuable to other people; when they have sex, they risk catching a disease or getting pregnant (in addition to many other emotional consequences). If possible, try to steer the negative consequences away from "you might get caught," and go to the deeper issues. If students get stuck, prod them to think about long-term consequences they could experience months or even years later.

Explain to the group that while disobeying God might seem to bring short-term benefits, in the long run, the person who sins always pays the price. In fact, it's been said that when a person breaks God's laws, God's laws break that person! Transition to the next step by explaining that each group member will have a chance today to choose one of God's Ten Commandments to obey more fully this week.

Option 2: Short-term Benefits. For this option, you will only need this book. Read the following story to the students:

Alex was new to Jefferson Middle School and wanted desperately to fit in. In her old school, she had been one of the most popular seventh-graders. But now that she had to move across town for her stepdad's job, she had to start all over making friends at her new school.

People didn't pay much attention to Alex at first. In fact, they would have entire conversations in front of her as if she were invisible. They would talk about other kids at school, usually saying mean things about how dumb or ugly those other kids were.

One day at lunch, a group of cheerleaders were talking in front of Alex about the girls involved with drama. They said they couldn't believe what geeks the drama girls were and that they wished they would transfer to another school. The next day at lunch, Alex happened to be in line at the cafeteria with a bunch of the drama girls. One of them mentioned one of the cheerleaders' names and said she wondered what she thought of their group. Alex piped in, "Oh, I know. I heard her yesterday. She and all her other cheerleader friends think you guys are geeks and wish you would transfer to another school."

All of the drama girls turned toward Alex. "Really?" one of them said. "What else did you hear?" Alex couldn't believe it. People were finally paying attention to her! She told them about how other groups, such as the dance team and the newspaper staff, also thought the drama group was a bunch of losers.

Ask your group members what Alex has gained by spreading this news. (Some answers would include acceptance and friends. Alex might have also felt that she had finally found a way to be acknowledged and accepted by telling the drama group what she had overheard other people say.) Now ask the students to think of what Alex will be facing a few months down the road. Sure, she's made friends, but once she runs out of information for the drama group, they'll get sick of her, or they'll get tired of hearing negative stuff from her all the time. They might even start to mistrust her, because if she shared information *with* them, she might be sharing information *about* them.

Summarize by explaining that while it often seems in the short run that there are some benefits to disobeying God's laws, if we look weeks or months down the line, our disobedience catches up with us. We pay a heavy price for just a few minutes of fame. On the other hand, while obeying God's voice and doing what He tells us to do in His Word won't make our life 100 percent smooth and easy, it will ultimately bring us a better life. Transition to the next step by explaining that each of the group members will have a chance today to choose one of God's Ten Commandments to obey more fully this week.

APPLY

Option 1: Dental Artists. For this option, you need tape, pens and paper. Ahead of time, tape the pieces of paper to one of the walls of the meeting room. You will need the same amount of paper as the number of volunteers that you are going to choose. Make sure that there is space between the papers.

Explain to the group members that the laws from Moses that Joshua obeyed were the Ten Commandments. Choose 10 volunteers, give each volunteer a pen, and have him or her stand in front of one of the pieces of paper on the wall. Explain that you are going to whisper one of the Ten Commandments into each person's ear, and when you do this, the volunteer needs to draw a picture of this commandment on his or her piece of paper. Here is the catch: the volunteer will have to hold the pen in his or her teeth. Allow the remaining students to gather around these "dental artists."

Start the game. When the volunteers are finished drawing, read the Ten Commandments found in Exodus 20:1-17 aloud. Have the group guess which of the Ten Commandments is represented in each picture. Next, have the stu-

Youth Leader Tip
When using materials such as markers and tape, paint or food, protect walls, floors, carpet and clothing by using drop cloths, pens that wash off and surface-friendly tape. Good supervision and ground rules can also keep the fun, fun (and the custodian happy).

dents stand by the piece of paper that best represents the commandment they need to work on the most in their own lives. Close in prayer, asking God to help the group members as they try to work on the commandment they chose. Also, thank God for the blessings that will come as they do this.

Option 2: Are You Off or On? For this option, you need a digital camera or recorder and a way to show what you have shot to the group. Ahead of time, record a water faucet running for 30 seconds, then show a hand turning it off so that no water can come out of it, and then record the water faucet doing nothing for 30 seconds.

As you start to show the clip to your group, explain that the more they obey what God has told them to do in the Bible, the more they are like this water faucet. God can work through them in the same way He did through Joshua. He also can bless people through them. God might even use them to share about their relationship with Jesus and invite others to have a relationship with Him as well. When the clip shows the hand turning off the water faucet, explain that when they disobey what God has told them to do, He can't work through them as well. Not only will they feel drier spiritually, but also others around them will not be able to experience God's blessings in the same way.

Give the group members a chance to examine their own hearts. Ask them to think about whether they are like the water faucet that has been turned on or the faucet that has been turned off. In other words, is their disobedience preventing God from working through them in the way that He wants to work? Give students a chance to confess any sins with which they may be struggling, and then thank God for His forgiveness.

REFLECT

The following short devotions are for the students to reflect on and answer during the week. You can make a copy of these pages and distribute to your class or download and print from **www.gospellight.com/uncommon/jh_listening_to_God.zip.**

1—THE LIVING WORD

Some people would say that a poem is nothing but black marks on white paper. And, if you look at a poem under a microscope, you will see that this is true—there is only paper and ink. But those who read the words of the poem and are moved by it find it to be more than just words on a page.

In the same way, you can pick up a Bible and just see it as scratches of ink on paper. If you don't read the words and think about what they say, you won't be able to hear God speaking to you through those words. If you don't apply what the Bible says to your life, it will not change you in any way.

Think about this for a moment. Have you ever read a verse of the Bible and felt as if God were speaking to you? Describe the situation.

_____

_____

_____

_____

_____

James 1:23-24 says, "Anyone who listens to the word but does not do what it says is like a man who looks at his face in a mirror and, after looking at himself, goes away and immediately forgets what he looks like." What do you think the author means?

_____

_____

_____

_____

Today, ask God to speak to you through His Word. He will!

2—HOW TO BE SUCCESSFUL

Want to be successful? Read Joshua 1:7. What did God tell the people to do to be successful wherever they went?

_____

_____

_____

_____

_____

To be successful, the people had to obey God's "law," which were the words He had given to Moses (we find these in the books of Genesis, Exodus, Leviticus, Numbers and Deuteronomy). To do that, they first had to know what the law said. How do we know what God wants us to do?

_____

_____

_____

_____

God has spoken to us in His Word, the Bible, and the more we obey what He says, the better off we will be. Reading His Word will teach us what to do! Write a short prayer asking God to help you read the Bible and follow what it says.

_____

_____

_____

_____

3—HEARING GOD SPEAK

As we discussed in this session, God has already spoken to us in His Word, the Bible, and we don't have to wonder what He is trying to say to us. Yet God speaks to us in other ways as well. If you could pick any way you wanted to communicate with God, what would it be?

_____

_____

_____

Why do some people find it hard to talk with God and hear from Him?

_____

_____

_____

_____

To talk with our friends, we have to spend time with them. We have to pick up the phone, or text them, or go visit them. How is this the same with God?

_____

_____

_____

_____

Today, spend some time reading the Bible, and as you do, remember that you are building a friendship with God. Then listen for Him to speak to you!

4—FINDING GOD

Looking for something? Read Jeremiah 29:13. According to this verse, we will find God when we:

- ❏ Spend time in church
- ❏ Spend time with Christian friends
- ❏ Seek Him with all our heart
- ❏ Write to Him on Facebook

What do you think it means to seek God with all your heart?

_____

_____

_____

_____

_____

Imagine that a friend has something to tell you that you have been dying to hear, and you know that this friend will be home at 7 PM. Will you wait until 9 PM to call? No! You will get on your cell phone and call or text that person right away. You will *seek* out that person so you can hear what he or she has to say. The same is true of God. So . . . what will you do this week to spend time regularly seeking God by reading the Bible?

_____

_____

_____

_____

_____

SESSION 2

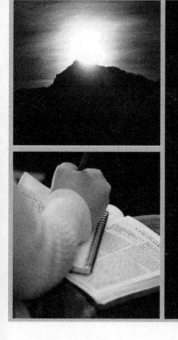

SEEKING GOD'S VOICE FOR GUIDANCE

THE BIG IDEA

We need to seek God's voice and ask for His direction and guidance in our lives each and every day.

SESSION AIMS

In this session, you will guide students to (1) be reminded things aren't always what they seem; (2) feel motivated to seek God's guidance regularly, especially for situations that are confusing and hard to understand; and (3) choose at least one area of their lives where they need to seek God's guidance this week.

THE BIGGEST VERSE

"The Israelites sampled their provisions but did not inquire of the LORD" (Joshua 9:14).

OTHER IMPORTANT VERSES

Joshua 5:13-6:27; 9:1-27

Note: Additional options and worksheets in 8^1/$_2$" x 11" format for this session are available for download at **www.gospellight.com/uncommon/jh_listening_to_God.zip**.

STARTER

Option 1: Taggers. For this option, you will need some large paper bags with eyeholes cut in them and several pairs of sunglasses. Ahead of time, ask a few group members to come early and stay hidden in a nearby room or office. Each person should get a paper bag and a pair of sunglasses.

Greet the group and then comment on the fact that it seems that there are a few students missing today. Explain that this is due to the fact they are part of the next game the group will be playing. Tell them that you are going to bring out some "taggers," and then have your volunteers come out with their bags and sunglasses on. Point to the volunteers and explain to the group that taggers are fellow students who are in disguise so the group can't figure out who they are. If any of them tag or touch a student, that person must join hands with the tagger and try to tag the remaining students. The last two people remaining who haven't been tagged are the winners.

Play the game in the largest open area available to you (gymnasium of your church, grass field, or if you're independently wealthy, the nearest sports stadium). When there are only two people remaining, end the game and congratulate these two winners. After this, ask students to guess who each of the taggers is. If your students guess a person's identity correctly, have the tagger remove his or her bag and sunglasses. Ask the person who guessed correctly how he or she could tell who it was.

Remind the group members that they are studying a series about hearing God's voice. Last time, we learned about a man named Joshua who understood that if he obeyed what God told him, things would go better for him. Today, we're going to check out another episode in Joshua's life. This time, Joshua was deceived and had a hard time looking past the disguises of another group of people. They didn't wear sunglasses and bags over their heads, but they did something even trickier. As we will see, Joshua learned a lesson the hard way about the importance of listening to God's voice.

Option 2: Pie Eating Contest. For this option, you will need several real pies, a few homemade tuna pies, a tarp, a long table, three chairs, blindfolds and a stopwatch. Ahead of time, make a few tuna pies by filling some pie tins with tuna and covering them with whipped cream. Before the meeting, lay out the tarps where the pie eating will take place. Put the long table and three chairs on the tarp. Have both the regular pies and the tuna pies ready to go.

Greet students and divide them into teams based on their favorite flavor of pie (apple, cherry and pumpkin could make three teams). Choose one volunteer from each team to come forward to eat a pie. Have the volunteers sit at the table, and then blindfold them. Bring out the regular pies and set one in front of each volunteer. Explain that each volunteer has 60 seconds to eat as much pie as he or she possibly can. After 60 seconds, call the end of the game. Congratulate the winner and ask for an additional volunteer from the teams who didn't win. Repeat the process for these two volunteers so that you have two finalists that are not from the same team.

Explain to the two blindfolded finalists that they are now in the pie-eating championships. You are going to put a pie in front of each person, and just as before, the winner will be the one who can eat the most pie in 60 seconds. Bring out the tuna pies and place them before the two blindfolded finalists. Say, "Ready, set, go!"

Depending on the finalists' level of adrenaline or their sense of taste and smell, it could take anywhere from 2 to 10 seconds for them to realize what they're eating. If a finalist wants to stop eating, allow him or her to do so. Otherwise, at the end of 60 seconds, call the end of the game. The finalist who lasts the longest is the winner.

Interview both volunteers, asking the following questions:

- How was this pie different from the first round?
- How did you feel when you realized you had tuna in front of you?
- Did you feel like I had tricked you?

Admit that you did indeed trick the volunteers, but that it was to make the point that things in life aren't always what they seem. What the contestants thought was a delicious pie was actually some smelly tuna. Today, the group members are going to find out about another episode in Joshua's life as he continues to learn how to hear God's voice. As we'll see, he learned the hard way that appearances can be deceiving and that it is important to check with God first before making an important decision.

MESSAGE

Option 1: Choose Your Gift. For this option, you will need a Bible and some wrapped gifts. Ahead of time, put together a group of gifts and wrap them. Some of the gifts should be bad, such as a cracked egg in a baggy, an onion, or an empty CD case. Wrap these gifts in beautiful wrapping paper and bows. A few of the gifts should be great, such as a gift certificate or any amount of money. Wrap these gifts in newspaper or other cheap paper. These gifts should look shabby on the outside.

Call five students who have had a birthday recently to come up to the front of the room. Figure out which student has a birthday closest to today and let him or her choose first from among the presents. Then have the student with the birthday second closest to today choose, and so on until all the gifts have been chosen. When everyone has a gift, let him or her unwrap it. Odds are that the students will choose the nicely wrapped gifts first, but if something else happens, modify the following discussion questions to fit whatever your students chose.

Ask the first few students why they chose the gift they did and how they felt about what they received. Next, ask the students who got the crummy looking gifts with the valuable prizes the following questions:

- What were you expecting?
- Why did you expect this?
- How were your gifts the same or different than what you expected?

Explain that we all are quick to judge things based on how they initially appear. Sometimes we are right, but many times we're very wrong. Explain that in the last session, we read how Joshua had just had a great military success against Jericho. By this time, Israel had become a victorious army, and other groups in the region were beginning to worry that they would be wiped out next. The kings of these small nations began to join forces. Choose one or two volunteers to read Joshua 9:1-27. Make sure the group members get the full picture of what happened in the story by explaining the following points:

- All the kings listed in this passage that banded together were rulers over small kingdoms scattered throughout the Promised Land.
- The Gibeonites decided to try a different tactic.
- The Gibeonites approached the Israelites dressed in the dirtiest, most patched-up clothes they could find and carried worn-out sacks and wineskins to make it seem as if they were from a faraway country.
- In truth, Gibeon was located just north of Jerusalem.
- The men lied about where they had come from and offered to become the servants of the Israelites if Joshua would agree to a peace treaty.
- Joshua and his followers "did not inquire of the LORD" (Joshua 9:14) and took the bait.

- Three days later, the Israelites found out that the Gibeonites were their neighbors. They wanted Joshua to attack the Gibeonites, but Joshua refused because he had taken an oath.
- So instead, the Isaelites made them their servants, primarily as woodcutters and water carriers for the community.[1]

Ask the students the following questions:

- How was what happened to the Israelites similar to what happened to the people who chose the beautifully wrapped gifts? (*They were fooled by how things looked because they didn't know the truth.*)
- How would you have felt if you had been tricked by the Gibeonites? (*Angry, frustrated, ashamed at allowing yourself to be tricked.*)
- How do you think the Gibeonites felt when they were able to fool Israel? (*Proud that their plan had worked out so well, relieved that they wouldn't be attacked next.*)
- If you were writing a newspaper article about what happened, what would be your headline? (*Allow students to answer.*)
- What do you think the leaders of the Israelites learned about hearing from God? (*If something seemed even the least bit confusing, or if they were the least bit unsure, they needed to ask God for guidance.*)
- What are some other times when it's good to seek God? (*Sometimes people aren't lying to us, but maybe circumstances are confusing, or two options seem equally good. In those times, we need to seek God's voice.*)
- Can you think of a time when it's not good to seek God? (*Uh . . . pretty much NO on that one. It's never a bad idea to seek God!*)

Conclude by stressing that it is important to listen carefully for God's voice, because He will always show us the truth.

Option 2: A Battle of Wits. For this option, you will need a Bible, a stick, a clear pitcher with water in it, the movie *The Princess Bride,* and a way to play the film to your group. Ahead of time, queue the scene where Vecini, the bald "bad guy," engages in a battle of the wits with the hero (dressed in all black). The scene ends when Vecini drinks the poison and falls over dead. You will also need to ask a few of your adult volunteers to come to the meeting ready to share two truths and one lie about themselves.

Read Joshua 9:1-27. Explain that Joshua had just experienced a great military success against Jericho, and this victory made the other nations in Canaan concerned that they would be attacked next. So they began to band together against the Israelites. The people of one nation called Gibeon, located just north of Jerusalem, decided to try to trick Joshua instead of fight against him. They sent a delegation with donkeys loaded with worn-out sacks, and the men put on patched sandals and old clothes. Everything gave the appearance that they had travelled a great distance.

The delegation told Joshua that they had come from a faraway country and that they wanted to make a peace treaty. The Israelites checked out their story, but they didn't ask God about it, and Joshua made the deal. Three days later, the Israelites found out that the Gibeonites were actually their neighbors. The people wanted Joshua to revoke the promise, but Joshua was bound by an oath. So he made the Gibeonites servants, primarily as woodcutters and water carriers for the community. The Gibeonites didn't complain.

Explain that from this story we learn three reasons why we need to seek God's guidance in our lives. The first is because *people deceive us*. At this point, have your adult volunteers share two truths and one lie about themselves. Let the students vote on which of the three statements is a lie, and then have each adult volunteer reveal the lie that he or she told. Continue by stating that the group members knew that these adults would be lying to them in one of their three statements, but this will not always be the case in real life. Sometimes people try to intentionally deceive us, like in the story of the Gibeonites, but at other times it's accidental. Either way, we need to hear from God, because only He will never lie to us.

Explain that a second reason why we need to seek God's guidance is because *circumstances deceive us*. Reread Joshua 9:9-13. Note to the group that the circumstances surrounding these so-called refugees from a distant country were deceptive—the bread was moldy, and their clothes and shoes were worn and dirty. No wonder the leaders of Israel concluded that they were from a faraway place. Place the stick in the clear pitcher of water. State that when the stick is placed in water, it looks as if it is bending. Now, we know it's not really bending, but the circumstances make it *look* like it is. So, once again, things around us can be confusing, which makes it all the more important we hear from God.

Continue by stating that a third reason why we need to seek God's guidance is because *we can deceive ourselves*. Reread Joshua 9:14 and explain that the men of Israel thought they could figure out the truth on their own, but they were wrong. Set up *The Princess Bride* scene by stating that you will be showing a scene from a movie where a man is trying to figure out the truth himself. However, as we will see, he is not as smart as he thinks his is, and he pays the ultimate price for his bad choice. The "bad guy" is the shorter bald man, while the "good guy" is the man wearing all black. They are in a battle of wits over the princess, who is wearing all red and remains blindfolded.

Play the scene for the group, and then conclude by sharing how this shows that even our own wits can be deceived, especially when we think we're invincible or smarter than everybody else. What we need to do is listen carefully for God's voice, because He will always show us the truth.

DIG

Option 1: Tough Decisions. For this option, you will need just this book. Explain to the group member that sometimes we, like the Israelites, are faced with some tough decisions and we don't know what to do. Give the group some examples, and let them decide what to do in the following activity.

Instruct the students to listen to the following statements you are going to read and then make a decision. If they choose response *A*, they must go to the right side of the room. If they choose response *B*, they need to go to the left side of the room. Read the following dilemmas one at a time, giving students a chance to explain after each one why they're standing where they are:

- If you were really short on money for the upcoming winter camp at church, you would:
  A. Miss church so you could babysit and save for it.
  B. Go to church anyway.

- If you were playing a computer game with your little brother, who was depressed, you would:
  A. Play like you normally do and wipe him out.
  B. Make a few extra mistakes so he could win.

- If your friend bought a new lime green backpack that you thought was totally ugly, you would:
  A. Say that you really liked it.
  B. Tell her the truth.

- If your family was starving for food and hadn't eaten all day, you would:
  A. Steal pancakes from a nearby restaurant so they could eat.
  B. Let everyone go hungry for a second day in a row.

- If you had a big science test tomorrow where your score would make the difference between a *C* and a *B* in the class, but a friend in crisis needed to talk to you, you would:
  A. Spend two hours talking to the friend instead of studying.
  B. Study, but ask her to call you back tomorrow when the test was done.

Explain that life can be filled with difficult choices, which is why we need God's voice in our lives. In which of these situations would it make sense to ask God for advice? Pretty much all of them—they're all very tricky.

Option 2: The Best Decision. For this option, you will just need this book. Read the following case study to your students:

Jordan was an eighth-grader in middle school. He had done well in his classes and had grown a ton in his faith. He had acted on every chance to share with his friends about church and all the cool things he got to do there, as well as what his relationship with Jesus meant to him.

But now that he was nearing the end of his eighth-grade year, he had to figure out what high school to attend. Most of his friends were continuing on in the nearby public high school, but that school was rumored to be pretty tough. They had installed metal detectors at the front doors, and a kid had gotten stabbed there last month. Most of his friends from church were going to a private Christian school 10 miles away. It cost more, and he would miss the chance to be around non-Christians, but the idea of having a class every day on the Bible seemed cool.

On a whim, Jordan had applied to a third school called Eastridge, the most academically challenging private school in his city. Because of his good grades and excellent recommendations from teachers, he was accepted. Eastridge cost a ton of money, and though his parents said they would pay for it if he wanted to go, he knew it would be hard on them. He also knew he would have more homework to do there, so it might be harder for him to play sports and go to youth group. On the other hand, it had such a great reputation that it would almost guarantee he could go to whatever college he wanted to attend.

Ask the group the following questions:

- What are the advantages for Jordan of going to the public school? What are the disadvantages?

- What would be the advantages of going to the private Christian school? What would be the disadvantages of going to that school?
- How about Eastridge, the challenging private school? What are the advantages and disadvantages for Jordan at that school?
- Who should Jordan talk to for some good advice about his decisions?
- What would you tell Jordan if he came to you for advice?
- Do you think you should give him advice if you haven't prayed about it first yourself? Why or why not?

Explain that all of these options have their advantages and disadvantages. It might be that Jordan would pray a bunch and still not know exactly what God wanted. Sometimes that happens, which means we have to rely on others and our own sense of what is right. Or maybe Jordan would pray and know totally what God wanted. Either way, the important thing is that Jordan prayed to make sure he wasn't missing out on God's plans.

APPLY

Option 1: Getting Rid of the Junk. For this option, you will need earplugs, pens or pencils, and copies of the handout "Getting Rid of the Junk" (found on the next page).

Hold up the earplugs and state that there are often things that occur in our lives that block out our ability to hear from God. In many ways, it is as if we are wearing earplugs. Distribute copies of the handout "Getting Rid of the Junk," and the pens and pencils. Explain that when we sense that we can't hear God's voice, we need to see if there is any junk in our "spiritual ears" that is blocking our communication.

Direct the group members' attention to the three items listed on the handout that keeps us from hearing God: pride, busyness and laziness. On a scale of 1 to 10—with 10 being a major problem and 1 being no big deal—they need to circle the number that best describes how each issue gets in their way. Then, under each number they have selected, they need to write why they circled that particular number.

Give the group members a few minutes to do this and then ask them to look at the bottom half of the handout. Have them write a prayer to God confessing their problems with these issues and asking for forgiveness and help. Close the time by praying that God will help them and open their spiritual ears so that they can hear Him.

GETTING RID OF THE JUNK

On a scale of 1 to 10, with 10 being a major problem and 1 being no big deal, circle the number that best describes how each of the following blocks your ears from hearing God. Then write why you circled that particular number.

PRIDE

1   2   3   4   5   6   7   8   9   10

Why I circled that number:

_____
_____
_____

BUSYNESS

1   2   3   4   5   6   7   8   9   10

Why I circled that number:

_____
_____
_____

LAZINESS

1   2   3   4   5   6   7   8   9   10

Why I circled that number:

_____
_____
_____

Now write a prayer to God, asking Him to clean out your ears so you can hear His voice all day long!

_____
_____
_____
_____

Option 2: Ripe or Unripe. For this option, you will need ripe and unripe fruit. Ideally, the unripe fruit should be either a different color than the ripe fruit, or a lot harder than the ripe fruit so the group will be able to tell the difference.

Explain that one area in which we need to hear God's voice is our relationship with our non-Christian friends. If we don't know where they are in regard to their relationship with God, it will be harder to know how to point them to Him. Hold up the ripe fruit. Explain that the fruit you are holding is "ripe" and ready to be eaten. In the same way, some of our friends are ready to hear the gospel and are ready to respond. Now hold up the unripe fruit. Explain that this type of fruit might be like other friends. They may not be as interested in hearing about Christ right now. This doesn't mean we should never talk about Jesus or church with them, but it may be harder for us to talk to these friends.

Divide the group in half. Have one half go to the right side of the room and one half go to the left. Point to the group in the left half of the room and ask them to think of one thing a person who was not ready to hear the gospel would say about church, God, the Bible or Christianity. Possible answers may include the following: "God doesn't really exist"; "All religions are the same"; "The Bible has lots of errors"; "Christianity doesn't make sense." After the group gives each idea, point to the right side of the room and have the students on this side tell you how they would respond to that statement or question. Repeat this several times, asking the left side of the room for statements and then asking the right side for appropriate responses.

Repeat this for the group on the right half of the room. Have the students come up with statements a person who is open to receiving Christ might say, such as, "Could I come to church sometime?" "Why do you read the Bible?" "How can you have so much joy even when everything around you stinks?" After each statement or question, have the group on the left half of the room come up with responses that fit ("Sure, you can come to church with me." "I read the Bible so I can know what God wants me to do in my life." "Christ gives us His joy, so we can be glad in any circumstance.")

Close in prayer, asking God to guide the students to know how to respond to those around them, whether they are ready or not ready to hear the gospel.

REFLECT

The following short devotions are for the students to reflect on and answer during the week. You can make a copy of these pages and distribute to your class or download and print from **www.gospellight.com/uncommon/jh_listening_to_God.zip.**

1—A GOOD PLAN

What's God's plan? Is it a good one? Check out Jeremiah 29:11.

When Mike was a four-year-old, he loved to visit his grandparents. They were so much fun, and they had their very own pool. Mike loved to play in the pool, but he had to wear a life vest because he didn't know how to swim. His grandparents were careful not to leave Mike alone near the pool. They also warned him to never go into the pool alone.

One day, Mike asked his grandparents if he could go in the pool, and they told him he had to wait. Mike decided that he could go by himself as long as he wore his life vest. He found the vest, but he wasn't quite sure how to zip it up. *Oh well*, he thought, *at least I have it on.*

Mike jumped into the deep end of the pool. When he hit the water, pop! His vest came right off, and he began to sink. Fortunately, his grandparents noticed that he had disappeared from the kitchen, and his grandfather was able to dive into the pool and save him. Mike never forgot that day. When he grew older, he could understand that everything his grandparents did—even in saying no—was to help and protect him.

How did Mike's grandparents show that they loved him?

_____

_____

_____

Have your parents ever said no when you asked them for something you really wanted? If so, what reason did they give for saying no?

_____

_____

_____

We need to believe that God loves us and that He wants the very best for us. Sometimes He says no to what we want because it would not be best for us.

2—GOOD INTENTIONS

Perhaps you think you have heard from God and have a pretty good idea of what He wants you to do. Then you set out to do it, and nothing works right. You begin to wonder what is going on.

It's like the story of the *Cat in the Hat*. It is the Cat's intention to entertain two children who are home alone on a rainy afternoon. But even though his intentions are good, everything goes wrong. He pulls out all sorts of objects, and soon the house is a wreck. It's chaos, and nothing is going according to plan. Then, just as the kids' mother arrives in the driveway and they think they will be grounded for the rest of their lives, the Cat takes out a machine that cleans up everything. He disappears just as the kids' mother walks in the front door.

Have you ever had an idea that you thought was wonderful but went very wrong? Explain what happened.

_____

_____

_____

What is the danger in thinking that what we want to do is best and not asking God? (Hint: Remember Joshua and the Gibeonites!)

_____

_____

_____

Sometimes we set out to do what we think God wants us to do. We have a plan, and then things start to go wrong, and we begin to wonder if we heard from God at all. What do we do? Well, we need to keep moving forward and asking God to help us. In the same way that the Cat got everything in place at just the right time, God will help us get to our goal—sometimes just at the right time.

3—A TOUGH SPOT

Is it getting hot in here? Read Daniel 3:13-23 to find out what happened to three young men who got into trouble because they *were* following God's plan.

Shadrach, Meshach and Abednego were in a tough spot. They could choose to bow down and worship a statue and live, or not bow down and be thrown into a heated furnace that would likely kill them. They knew that God's Word had said they were not to worship anyone but God.

So they chose to obey God and not obey the king. They didn't know whether God would save them from death or not. They only knew that they had to obey God.

Did Shadrach, Meshach and Abednego fry and die? What happened to them?

_____

_____

_____

When you are trying to obey God and things start to go wrong, what do you do next?

- ❏ Grab a gallon of chocolate chunk ice cream and eat the whole thing.
- ❏ Run for the nearest exit sign, screaming, "I didn't sign up for this!"
- ❏ Keep obeying God and ask for His help.
- ❏ Tune out and go play your favorite computer game.

Remember that when God asks us to do something, He will always help us. We need to keep going and allow Him to help us finish the task.

4—POP QUIZ!

Time for a little pop quiz. Circle true if you think the statement is correct and false if you think the statement isn't correct:

God loves you and has an awesome plan for your life.	True	False
God will only speak to you if you are obeying Him perfectly.	True	False
You can know you are obeying God if nothing bad ever happens in your life.	True	False
When you follow God, you *will* go through hard situations.	True	False
God will be there to help you through those tough times.	True	False

We don't have to do everything perfect to hear God's voice and know what He wants for us. We just have to take the time to listen to Him. What are three ways God can speak to us?

_____

_____

_____

Today, take some time to just be quiet and listen to God. He may want to share something with you right now!

SEEKING GOD'S VOICE FOR HIS VISION

THE BIG IDEA

We need to seek God's voice and ask Him to give us His vision for our future.

THE BIGGEST VERSE

"As for all the inhabitants of the mountain regions from Lebanon to Misrephoth Maim, that is, all the Sidonians, I myself will drive them out before the Israelites. Be sure to allocate this land to Israel for an inheritance, as I have instructed you" (Joshua 13:6).

LESSON AIMS

In this lesson, you will guide students to (1) realize the benefits of knowing where they are headed in the future; (2) feel encouraged that God involves them in His plans for their futures; and (3) seek to hear what God might be saying to them about their futures.

OTHER IMPORTANT VERSES

Exodus 24:12-13; 33:7-11; Deuteronomy 3:28; Joshua 13:1-7; Psalm 116:1; Jeremiah 29:11-13; 33:3; Jonah 1:1-4; Matthew 6:25-27; John 3:16; 14:6; Romans 3:23; 6:23; 1 John 1:9; Revelation 3:20

Note: Additional options and worksheets in 8^1/$_2$" x 11" format for this session are available for download at **www.gospellight.com/uncommon/jh_listening_to_God.zip**.

STARTER

Option 1: Spin Relay. For this option, you will need some baseball bats and some room to run.

Greet the students and divide them into teams of 10 to 15. Give each team a baseball bat. Explain that this is a relay race. One at a time, the team members are to run down to the opposite end of the room and pick up their team bat. The team members will then place the end of the handle on their forehead. While keeping the bat in this position, they will lean down facing the ground so that they are crouching with the bat's handle at their forehead and the other end of the bat about one inch above the ground. In this position, the team members will spin their body around 10 times, making sure to keep the handle of the bat at their forehead and the other end near the ground.

Once the team members have finished spinning 10 times, they will run back to their team and tag the next person in line. The next person *cannot* go until the person has tagged his or her hand. You might want to demonstrate the movements that the students will be performing so that they know what you are talking about. When everyone is clear on the instructions, start the race. After the relay race is finished, pronounce a winner based on which team finished first. After the room stops spinning for your students, lead them in the following discussion:

- How are you feeling?
- Was this game harder or easier than you thought it would be?
- What made it hard to head back to your team and tag the next player's hand?

Explain that it is frustrating to know where we're supposed to go but not be able to get there. Fortunately, God never leaves us in the dark. Today, we will learn that when we hear God's voice, He will not only show us where we are headed but also what we need to do to get there.

Option 2: A Puzzling Game. For this option, you will need several 50- to 75-piece puzzles. Each puzzle should be significantly different in color, shape and design from the others. Ahead of time, mix together all the puzzle pieces from the different boxes.

Greet the students and divide them into as many small groups as you have puzzles. Explain that they will be playing a game in which each group will try to be the first one to complete their puzzle. The twist to this game is that each group will have a pile of pieces, but only some of them will be from their own puzzle, while the rest will be from other puzzles. This means that each group will need to run around to the other groups and take any puzzle pieces that they think belong to their puzzle. Each group will have its own puzzle's box top, so they will know what the completed puzzle should look like. If anyone hides another group's pieces, that group will be automatically disqualified.

Play some rowdy background music as the students are running around looking for their own small-group pieces. When one group has finished its puzzle, stop the game and lead the following discussion:

- What made this game challenging? (*Allow students to answer.*)
- How would it have been different if you hadn't seen your own puzzle box top? (*It would have been much harder, if not impossible, for the groups to find their own puzzle pieces if they didn't know the end goal.*)
- In general, how many of you prefer to know the end goal when you're playing a game or trying to do something? (*Pretty much everyone will agree with you on this one.*)

Explain that one way we can know the end goal of where we're headed is to hear God's voice. As we will see today, when we hear God's voice, He will not only show us where we're headed but also what we need to do to get there.

MESSAGE

Option 1: Trash Can Ball. For this option, you will need a Bible, a few trash cans and many balls (like the cheap 99 cent ones they sell at stores). Ahead of time, talk to a handful of students and ask them to be part of the game. They will come forward when their number is called, but they will not throw any balls when they are asked to do so.

Divide your group into teams of no more than 12 people. Have all the teams line up and face each other. If you have two teams, that will be fairly easy. If you have three teams, they should form a triangle with an open space in between; four teams becomes a square; five becomes a pentagon; six becomes a hexagon—you get the idea.

Put all the balls in the center of your geometric shape of teams and give each team a trash can. Number off each team member (from 1 to 10) so that each team has a #1 person, #2 person, and so on. Explain that you are going to call out a few numbers. If one of the team members' numbers is called, that person must pick up a ball from the center and toss it into his or her own team's trash can from where he or she is standing. That player cannot move any closer. If the team member misses the trash can, he or she can run to pick up that same ball again and re-throw it or pick up a different ball.

Once all the balls are in the trash cans, the team members must return to their lines. You will need to put all the balls back in the center, call out some more numbers and repeat the process again. Keep track of which team collects the most balls. Make sure you don't stop the game until it becomes obvious to everyone that those students you secretly talked to ahead of time aren't playing the game according to your instructions.

Toward the end of the game, call out more and more numbers at the same time so more and more students end up in the center playing area. When you're done, pronounce the winning team and have everyone return to his or her seat. Ask the winning team what their secret was for winning the game. Ask the rest of the group why they seemed to get frustrated with the other team members during the game. Some answers could be, "They didn't throw the balls into the trash cans." "They didn't seem to really be playing for our team." "They just stood there." At this point, explain that you secretly asked these people ahead of time to play the role they did so that no one resents them for their actions.

Continue by stating that it is very frustrating when we're working toward a goal and we ask people to help, but they won't do it. Ask the group if they think God ever feels that way—that He speaks to us and asks us to do things, but we don't do them. Explain that today we will be studying one more example from Joshua's life about how we can hear God's voice. Read Joshua 13:1-7. Explain that this chapter in Joshua represents a major shift in Israel's identity. Instead of being a people *fighting* for the land, the Israelites became a people *living* in the land. Ask the following questions:

- According to Joshua 13:1-7, what was God's job? (*To drive out people before the Israelites and make sure they received the land God had promised them.*)
- What was Joshua's job? (*To divide the land as God had specified.*)
- What do you think would have happened if Joshua had not done what God said? (*God would have found another way, but it would have taken more time. In addition, Joshua would have missed out on some of the blessings of obeying God.*)
- Did God really *need* Joshua? (*No, but He did want Joshua to be part of His plan. In the same way, God doesn't need us to accomplish His goals—*

He loves us and chooses to work through us so that we can have the op-
portunity to be part of His plans.)
- How does this relate to the ball game we just played? (*The people who
  went to the center of the room and just stood there didn't stop their teams
  from winning, but they sure made it more difficult for them.*)
- If God is God, why does He involve us at all? (*This is a great question,
  and the answer is somewhat of a mystery. Probably the best answer is that
  He loves us and wants us to grow through the experience as we cooperate
  with Him. It's kind of like "on the job training" versus just reading a book
  about something. We learn much more by doing than just observing.*)[1]

Conclude by reiterating that God uses us in His plans because He loves us
and wants us to learn to rely on Him and hear His voice. We miss out on His
blessings when we ignore His voice or choose to take a different course.

Option 2: Our Slice of the Pie. For this option, you will need a Bible, some pies,
a knife, plastic plates, napkins and forks. Introduce this message by reading
Joshua 13:1-7. Call attention to the fact that this passage begins with the words
"When Joshua was old and well advanced in years." Time has passed, and the
Israelites have gone from an army conquering the land to residents living in the
land. Now, Joshua is dividing up the land for the different tribes.

Continue by stating that this passage reveals a few important points about
why we need to listen to God. First (and most obvious) is that listening to God
reveals *what He is going to do in our lives.* Reread Joshua 13:1-6 and point out
that it was God who would be providing the land to the Israelites. Hold up the
pies. Explain that it would be like God saying to us that He was going to provide these pies. We didn't make them or buy them—they came directly from
God. That is how most of life is. God is usually the one who does the bulk of
the work, but He also wants to include us.

State that a second reason to listen for God's voice is that it shows us how
God *wants us to respond.* Reread Joshua 13:6-7 and explain that although God
was providing the land, Joshua's job was to divide it up as He had specified. Pick
up the knife and state that it is as if God had handed a knife to Joshua and said,
"Here, you take what I've provided and do what I tell you to do with it." God
could have found some other way to divide the land, but Joshua and the people
would have missed out on some of the blessings that come from obeying God.

At this point, divide the pie up among your students as a tangible (and
yummy) object lesson of the difference between what God does (which is most

of the work) and our response (which is to obey what God wants us to do and generally play a much smaller part in the equation than God).

DIG

Option 1: Baby Steps. For this option, you will need a whiteboard and a whiteboard marker. Ahead of time, contact the parent (or parents) of a young toddler who is just learning to walk (probably a child around one year old). Ask the parent(s) if he or she can bring the child to your meeting for the following illustration. (If not, have the parent film the child taking a few unsteady steps, or look on YouTube for a similar clip.)

Begin by stating that any time we hear from God and decide to do what He wants us to do, we grow in our faith. Have the parent(s) bring the young child up near the front of the room (or start the clip), and then ask him or her to get the child to take a few steps, however faltering those steps may be. Explain that this child is only going to learn to walk by trying and sometimes falling. Notice how this child's parent(s) is close by, just waiting to applaud when he or she takes a few steps as well as to encourage the child when he or she stumbles. As this little one tries to walk, his or her muscles will grow even stronger.

Explain that the same thing is true when it comes to God and us. He wants us to grow. He is waiting right there to celebrate with us when we succeed as well as to encourage us when we fall. If we spend our whole life just sitting on the couch, we will never grow. It's only when we step out and try something new—such as by listening to God and obeying His voice—that our faith walk gets stronger.

Ask the students what they feel God wants them to do in the future, and make a list of these on the whiteboard. Next, ask the group how they think they can grow as they do each of these things. As the students give their answers, write next to each item the ways they can grow as they follow God. Point to the list and ask if there is anything on this list that scares them. Also ask if anything is exciting to them. Have them share the reasons why.

Explain to the group that once we hear from God about our future, the choice is up to us. We can either sit around and do nothing, or we can step out in faith and grow some spiritual muscles.

Option 2: The Choice. For this option, you will need just this book. Read the following story to your students:

By Wednesday at summer camp, Kelly was sure she knew what God was calling her to do. He wanted her to start a campus Bible study at her middle school. As an eighth-grader, she knew lots of people at the school, but she didn't think any of them were Christians. *Oh well,* she told herself. *I guess I'll just give it a shot.*

It took her a few months to spread the word, but the time finally arrived when she felt she had enough of a response to attempt a first meeting after school. Five minutes before that first Wednesday meeting, Kelly was nervous. She knew she was doing what God wanted her to do, but she was afraid she would be all alone. To her surprise, 16 other students showed up. Even more surprising to Kelly, they all came back the next week—and the week after that, and the week after that.

By the spring, the club had grown even larger. Kelly was the president, but she was working hard at training her seventh-grade vice president so he could keep the club going after she graduated.

In March, Kelly decided to try out for the school play. She couldn't believe it when she found out that she had been cast in the lead part. There was one problem, however: all practices were mandatory, and they practiced every Monday and Wednesday after school. So Kelly had to make a decision: she could either hand over the leadership of the Bible club to her vice president, or she could turn down the lead in the school play. Kelly asked several friends for advice on what to do, but they all told her different things.

Discuss the following questions based on this story with the group:

- If Kelly had come to you for advice, what would you have told her to do?
- What would you have chosen if you were in Kelly's place?
- Kelly's club was pretty successful, but many times when junior-highers feel called to lead Christian clubs, not many other kids show up. Does that make them less successful than Kelly's club? Why or why not?

Now read the ending of the story:

Kelly decided that God hadn't yet released her from leading the Christian club. He still wanted to work through her, so she told the drama teacher that she would really like to be the lead but couldn't make it to the practices.

The drama teacher thought about it for a day and then called Kelly at home. "Kelly," she said, "I've decided to change the practice schedule to Tuesdays and Thursdays so you can make it. Would you like the lead?"

Kelly couldn't believe it. She could do both the Christian club and the school play! This was too good to be true.

Explain that God honored Kelly's willingness to listen to His voice by changing the drama practices, but that doesn't always happen. Ask the group what they would have told Kelly if things hadn't worked out this way and she later regretted the decision to lead the club. What was He trying to teach Kelly through this? Conclude by stating that it is important to keep listening to God. Although He is working in our lives, it may take some time to see the results.

APPLY

Option 1: Short Scenes. For this option, you will need five students who will be in a simple skit. Meet with the volunteers ahead of time to practice the skit. Designate one student to be "God," another to be "Sin," another to be "Jesus," and a girl and guy to be "people." Make sure that your "God" and "Jesus" actors are physically bigger than your "Sin" actor, so that your group will have a more vivid image in their minds.

Begin by stating that all of us have wondered at one time or another what is going to happen to us when we die. Although it's hard to believe, all of us are going to die at some point—and some of us sooner than others. For this reason, you want the group to think about the following question: "If you got in a car accident on the way to school tomorrow, do you know where you would end up?"

State that if anyone is unsure about his or her answer, or if anyone doesn't like the answer he or she came up with, you would like that person to pay special attention to the drama that is about to be performed. Call up your five volunteers and have them act out the following scenes, making sure you narrate the action so the audience can follow along:

- Scene One: The student you have introduced as "God" is hanging out with the two you have designated as "people." Explain that this scene represents the Garden of Eden, where Adam and Eve had an unblocked relationship with God.

- Scene Two: "Sin" walks out and stands between the people and God with his arms out, making it impossible for the people to reach God. State that when "sin" walked into the picture, it blocked the people's relationship with God.

- Scene Three: "Jesus" walks into the scene and extends His hands like a cross. Explain that God decides to do something to make it possible for the people to have a relationship with Him again, so He sends His Son, Jesus. The crucifixion and the resurrection break the block of sin's power to keep the people away from God. All they have to do now is ask Jesus to be their Savior and to take over their lives, and then they have access once again to God. Have the two "people" hug Jesus, who then bumps "Sin" out of the way and behind Him so that the people can go back to God.

Each of these scenes should be only about 10 seconds long and are intended to flow into each other seamlessly. When the drama is finished, read at least some of the following Scripture passages: Romans 3:23; 6:23; John 3:16; 14:6 and 1 John 1:9. When you are done, invite students who have never received Jesus into their lives to do so now. Make sure you have some Bibles handy to give out. Write down the students' names, phone numbers and email addresses so that you can follow up with them in the next week.

Option 2: God's Dreams for Me. For this option, you will need copies of "God's Dreams for Me" (found on the next page). Begin by stating that back in the 1960s, Dr. Martin Luther King, Jr., felt that he knew what God was calling him to do. Ask if anyone in the group knows what his dream was, and then read the following portion of one of the most famous speeches he gave:

> I say to you today, my friends, that in spite of the difficulties and frustrations of the moment I still have a dream. It is a dream deeply rooted in the American dream.
>
> I have a dream that one day the nation will rise up and live out the true meaning of its creed: "We hold these truths to be self-evident; that all men are created equal."
>
> I have a dream that one day on the red hills of Georgia the sons of former slaves and the sons of former slave owners will be able to sit down together at the table of brotherhood.

GOD'S DREAMS FOR ME

I think God's dreams for me might be the following:

In my relationship with Him . . .

_____

_____

_____

_____

_____

In the way I serve Him . . .

_____

_____

_____

_____

In my relationship with my family . . .

_____

_____

_____

_____

In my relationships with my friends . . .

_____

_____

_____

_____

In other areas of my life . . .

_____

_____

_____

_____

I have a dream that one day even the state of Mississippi, a desert state sweltering in the heat of injustice and oppression, will be transformed into an oasis of freedom and justice.

I have a dream that my four children will one day live in a nation where they will not be judged by the color of their skin but by the content of their character.

I have a dream today . . .[2]

Now ask the group the following questions:

- How do you feel as you hear these words?
- If you had been an African-American living in states like Georgia and Mississippi during this time, how would you have felt?
- In what ways does having a dream for the future help us to move forward for causes such as this?
- Do you know what dreams God has for you in the next month, the next summer or the next year?

Distribute copies of "God's Dreams for Me." Invite the group members to spend at least five minutes a day for the next week praying and seeking God to find out what He might be telling them about each of the areas listed on the handout. If they already know where God wants them to go, have them go ahead and write it down. Ask the students to bring their handouts back the following week so they can share what they heard from God. Close in prayer, asking God to give all of your students' ears to hear God's dreams for their lives.

REFLECT

The following short devotions are for the students to reflect on and answer during the week. You can make a copy of these pages and distribute to your class or download and print from **www.gospellight.com/uncommon/jh_listening_to_God.zip.**

1—CAN YOU HEAR ME NOW?

There was a commercial from a cell phone company that aired some time ago with a guy that constantly went from place to place asking the person on the other end of the line, "Can you hear me *now*?" Sometimes, that's how you might feel about God. You dial in the prayers, but you're not certain if He has heard.

In such times, you can rest assured that God has heard you. As Psalm 116:1 says, "I love the LORD, for he heard my voice . . . he turned his ear to me." Sometimes, the problem might be that you didn't recognize that God was speaking to you. For this reason, it is important to get into the *habit* of regularly talking to God and listening to Him. This means setting aside a special time each day for prayer. Try to find a place that is quiet and where you can be alone.

During your time with God, read your Bible and ask God to speak to you. Talk to Him and write down anything you think He is saying to you. At first, it will be a little bit hard to recognize God's voice, but just like everything else in life, the more you practice, the better you will be able to hear Him.

What things tend to get in the way of having a daily prayer time?

_____

_____

_____

What would you need to do to get past these obstacles?

_____

_____

_____

Remember, you are not alone. God wants to be with you even more than you want to be with Him! He can't wait to be with you.

2—I KNOW YOU

We hear a lot about Moses in the Bible. He was always talking to God as he led the Israelites, and he saw God do a lot of miracles. While Moses was alive, his helper Joshua was not in the spotlight, but he was always a part of what Moses was doing. Read the following verses. Write down what is happening in this Scripture, and then write down what Joshua was doing in the background:

Exodus 24:12-13

_____

_____

_____

Exodus 33:7-11

_____

_____

_____

As Moses was leading the people, Joshua was learning how to talk to and listen to the Lord. When Moses was old and ready to die, God told him to "commission Joshua, and encourage and strengthen him, for he will lead this people across and will cause them to inherit the land that you will see" (Deuteronomy 3:28). Not only did Joshua become the next leader, but he was the one who led the Israelites into their new home God had promised to them! God chose Joshua because they were friends. He wants to have that same friendship with you.

3—THE CHOICE

When God speaks to you and tells you what He wants you to do, you have a choice to make. You can choose to obey Him, or you can choose to disobey Him. Even if you pretend you can't hear God and decide to do nothing, believe it or not, you have just made a choice—and not the best choice.

A man named Jonah found this out the hard way. Read Jonah 1:1-3. When God spoke to Jonah, what did he do?

☐ Said, "Yes, Lord!" and hurried on over to Nineveh.
☐ Took a slow caravan over to Nineveh, stopping in several interesting tourist spots along the way.
☐ Took a ship headed in the opposite direction.
☐ Said, "I can't hear You!" and visited the shops in Joppa.

Now read Jonah 1:4. What happened because of Jonah's choice?

_____

_____

_____

Did his choice only affect him? What does this tell you about not obeying God's voice?

_____

_____

_____

You probably know the end of the story. The sailors threw Jonah overboard, where a big fished swallowed him. Three days later, the fish upchucked Jonah on a beach, where God again told him to go to Nineveh. This time Jonah realized it wasn't a good idea to mess with God and went to the city. Take a lesson from Jonah and save yourself—and maybe even other people in your life—some trouble. If you hear God telling you to do something, go do it!

4—KNOCK, KNOCK

Did I hear a knock on the door? Check out Revelation 3:20 to see who it is.

Every day after school, you go over to your friend Troy's house and shoot hoops. It's something that the two of you have been doing since school started, and you look forward to spending this time with your friend. Then one day, Troy tells you that he is too busy to shoot hoops that day. "No problem," you say, knowing that the two of you will just get together again tomorrow.

As the weeks go by, however, Troy is busy more and more, and the two of you spend less time together after school. How does this make you feel?

_____

_____

_____

Two weeks later, you find out from another friend that the reason Troy has been so "busy" is that his parents gave him a new Xbox game, and he has been playing it every day. Now how do you feel?

_____

_____

_____

God wants to meet with you each day. He is standing at the door and knocking! How do you think He feels when things get in the way of you speaking to Him regularly?

_____

_____

_____

Take a few moments to talk to God and let Him know that you do want to spend time with Him. Ask Him to help you do this. He will!

SEEKING GOD'S VOICE FOR STRENGTH

THE BIG IDEA

We need to seek God's voice so we can receive the strength we need to overcome the obstacles that confront us.

SESSION AIMS

In this session, you will guide students to (1) realize they need more than their own strength; (2) feel motivated to increase their strength by hearing from God; and (3) commit to spend time with God daily so they can be filled with His strength more regularly.

THE BIGGEST VERSE

"One night the Lord spoke to Paul in a vision: 'Do not be afraid; keep on speaking, do not be silent. For I am with you, and no one is going to attack and harm you, because I have many people in this city'" (Acts 18:9-10).

OTHER IMPORTANT VERSES

Nehemiah 5:13; Luke 18:1-8; Acts 13:46-52; 18:5-17; Romans 7:14-25; 8:11,38-39; 2 Corinthians 11:9; Philippians 1:21,24; 4:4-15; 1 Thessalonians 3:6; 1 Timothy 4:12

Note: Additional options and worksheets in 8¹/₂" x 11" format for this session are available for download at **www.gospellight.com/uncommon/jh_listening_to_God.zip**.

STARTER

Option 1: United We Are Strong. For this option, you will only need your students. Greet your group members and then have the girls move to one side of the room and the guys to the other. Explain that the group will be playing a game—guys versus girls. Have the guys come to the center of the room and get in a huddle on the floor. They should link arms, legs, hands, whatever. They must get as close as they can and make sure they are holding on to each other. Ask the girls to try to pull the boys apart. Each guy must try to stay linked to at least one other guy on his team.

Before the game starts, let the girls know they must work alone. Then, after a few minutes, yell out that the girls have to work in pairs. A few minutes later, call out that they have to work in triplets. Congratulate the last two guys left. Repeat the process, but this time have the girls get in the tight huddle on the floor while the guys do the pulling. Afterward, ask the students if it made a difference to have someone help. Was it easier or harder to pull with help?

Explain that we often try to do things on our own, but it doesn't work as well as when we rely on other sources of strength to help us. Today, the group will be continuing this series on hearing God's voice. They will learn about someone who has given them more strength than they would ever have on their own.

Option 2: Stand Together. For this option, you will need only this book.

Greet students and divide them into groups of approximately 6 to 8 each (if your group is smaller than 12, just divide it into 2 equal groups). Have the tallest person in each group come forward. Make sure they have plenty of space around them. Ask them to stand on one foot while bending their other leg behind them for as long as possible. Tell the other players that if it appears their player is starting to sway and fall, any team member from that group can come and help that person stand. But here's the deal: the helper teammates have to stand on one foot and bend their other leg behind them as well. For example, let's say two team members run up to help the first person. When those three look like they're about to fall, a few other team members can come up and help steady everyone, but they all have to stand on one foot as well.

Continue by stating that if at any time even one team member falls or puts his or her other foot down, the whole team is out. Because any number of people can run up at any time, each team might want to have some kind of strategy so that their team will last as long as possible. Play this game a few times, allowing groups to get a feel for the most effective strategy. If your students seem to be able to stand on one foot longer than you'd like, make them close their eyes for several seconds at a time. This will make it much harder for them.

After the game is over, lead the following discussion:

- For those who were the first team players up there, how did it feel? Did your other team members come in right when you needed their help, or were they too early or too late?
- For those who were waiting to rush in and help, what kind of clues were you looking for to know when to rush in and help?
- Do you think you last longer when you try to do things on your own or when others help you?

Explain that even the most helpful group of people will sometimes let us down. However, as we continue our series today on hearing God's voice, we will discover someone who will never let us down. In fact, He will give us more strength than we could ever imagine.

MESSAGE

Option 1: Voice of Strength. For this option, you will need a Bible, some heavy item (such as bags of food or boxes of books), a scene from a popular television show and a way to show it to your group. Ahead of time, find a five-minute scene from the show that is known among your students. Ideally, you will be looking for a scene that has a lot of dialogue that is split evenly between a few characters. Count the number of characters who appear in the scene, as that will be the number of small groups you will have. Have the scene ready to play before the meeting.

Separate students into as many groups of six to eight people as you have characters in the scene that you are going to play (depending on the size of your overall group, you might need to assign the same character to more than one group). Assign each character on the television show to a team. Ask each team to choose the student who seems to be the strongest and to designate him or her as the "carrier." The carrier must stay just outside of arm's reach of the rest of the group.

Hand the carrier a few of the heavy items that you prepared for the meeting. Explain to the carrier that it is his or her job to hold these items the entire time the group watches a scene from a television show. However, each time their team's character speaks in the show, anyone from that team can take a few quick steps over to his or her carrier and help that person hold the items. As soon as their character is finished speaking, the helpers must let go of the items. Play the scene from the television show. If it is too easy for a certain group, give its carrier an additional bag or box.

When the scene is over, the carriers can put their items down. Ask the carriers if they began to love the voice of their groups' television character because it meant that they would get some help in the form of additional strength. Explain that in the last three lessons, the group has been studying about Joshua and how he heard God's voice. However, today they will be learning about another man in the Bible named Paul. Just like the team carriers, Paul learned that a voice could give him the strength he needed.

Explain that Paul had gone to several cities around the Mediterranean Sea and told everyone there about Jesus. In our story today, he had just left Athens and headed to Corinth (yes, as in the book of Corinthians). Read Acts 18:5-11 and state that Silas and Timothy brought good news to Paul about the church at Thessalonica (see 1 Thessalonians 3:6) as well as some money from the church at Philippi (see 2 Corinthians 11:9; Philippians 4:4-15). As a result of receiving the money, Paul was able to devote himself entirely to preaching the gospel instead of having to find a job, as was often his practice.

Explain that Corinth wasn't the first city where Paul faced opposition from the Jews for speaking about Jesus. The same thing had happened to him at Pisidian Antioch in Acts 13:46-52. However, in both Corinth and Antioch, the Jews' rejection of Paul and his message motivated him to spend more time with non-Jews, or the people who were known as the Gentiles. Shaking out his clothes was an act that symbolized his frustration at the Jews' opposition as well as a freedom from responsibility for them (see Nehemiah 5:13). Interestingly, one of Paul's first converts was Crispus, the leader of the synagogue, which was one of the key places of worship for the Jews.

State that a key piece of background information in helping us to better understand the passage is that on both Paul's Galatian and Macedonian journeys, he had begun with a good response from the citizens of the cities only to be forced later to leave them. It is likely that Paul was wondering if this very same thing was going to happen in Corinth, a city where he was starting to see some results. One night, God gave Paul a vision, encouraging him to be bold and to keep on speaking the gospel. Not only would God be with him, but other believers in the city would support him. As a result, Paul stayed there for 18 months.

Explain that Paul needed the strength he received from hearing God's voice. Read Acts 18:12-17. Sure enough, the Jews attacked Paul in court. However, Gallio, a Roman leader who had a reputation for being fair, decided not to get involved. His job was to judge civil and criminal cases, not to help settle religious disputes, and he commanded the Jews to settle the matter for themselves.[1] This meant that Christianity was not a violation of Roman law. This command gave Paul and others the freedom to preach about the gospel.

After explaining the story, discuss the following questions:

- How do you think Paul would have felt when he appeared before Gallio if he hadn't heard from God?
- How did hearing from God make a difference in the way he felt when he stood before Gallio?

Conclude by stating that this story shows us that hearing from God can give us all the strength we need just when we need it.

Option 2: Act It Out. For this option, you will need copies of "Act It Out" (found on the next two pages). Ahead of time, choose three people to play the parts of Jessica, Krista and God. Give the actors a chance to practice the skit before the meeting.

Introduce the skit to your group and have your actors perform part one. When they are finished, ask the group the following questions:

- What was Krista's problem? (*She was frustrated with her mom's boyfriend.*)
- What did Jessica do well? (*She listened, asked good questions and seemed to care.*)

Next, have the group members watch the same scene again, but this time there will be a twist. Have the same two actors, plus the person playing the part of God, act out part two. When they're done, ask the group what was the difference between the two scenes. (The answer is that in the second scene, Jessica heard from God, which gave her the strength to pray in public for Krista.)

Explain that many times we act just like non-Christians. If we're not hearing from God and relying on Him for strength, we might do some "nice things," just like Jessica did in the first scene. There is nothing she did that any other nice person wouldn't have done. It was only in the second scene when Jessica listened to God and let Him fill her with strength that she was bold enough to pray with Krista.

Read Acts 18:5-11. Explain that Paul had gone on several missionary journeys around the Mediterranean Sea, telling everyone he met about Jesus. In our

 ACT IT OUT

CHARACTERS

Jessica
Krista
God (part two only)

PART ONE

Jessica: Hey, Krista, you look kind of bummed today.

Krista: Is it that obvious? It's my mom's boyfriend. He's always over at our house and I'm just sick of him.

Jessica: Bummer. What does he do that makes you so frustrated?

Krista: Well, he tells me what to do, like he's my dad or something. He's not. He's not even related to me at all. Plus he smokes cigarettes all the time; so not only does he stink, but our whole house does too.

Jessica: How lame. What kinds of things does he tell you to do?

Krista: To clean my room, to study more, to be nicer to my mom.

Jessica: Well, have you tried talking to your mom about it?

Krista: Every time I bring it up, she just says I need to be quiet. She tells me that there aren't a lot of men who want to date a woman who has three teenage kids, so I better be nice to him.

Jessica: It doesn't sound like she's listening to you very well then.

Krista: Nope, all she cares about is herself. She's supposed to be my mom and take care of me, not be so wrapped up in her gross boyfriend.

Jessica: I'm sorry you have to go through this. Maybe we could talk more about it tomorrow after soccer practice.

Krista: Okay, I'd like that.

Jessica and Krista walk off together talking about all the homework they have. Scene ends.

PART TWO

Jessica: Hey, Krista, you look kind of bummed today.

Krista: Is it that obvious? It's my mom's boyfriend. He's always over at our house and I'm just sick of him.

Jessica: Bummer. What does he do that makes you so frustrated?

Krista: Well, he tells me what to do, like he's my dad or something. He's not. He's not even related to me at all. Plus he smokes cigarettes all the time; so not only does he stink, but our whole house does too.

Jessica: How lame. What kinds of things does he tell you to do?

Krista: To clean my room, to study more, to be nicer to my mom.

Jessica: Well, have you tried talking to your mom about it?

Krista: Every time I bring it up, she just says I need to be quiet. She tells me that there aren't a lot of men who want to date a woman who has three teenage kids, so I better be nice to him.

Jessica: It doesn't sound like she's listening to you very well then.

Krista: Nope, all she cares about is herself. She's supposed to be my mom and take care of me, not be so wrapped up in her gross boyfriend.

God: Jessica, you need to pray for Krista.

Jessica: (To God) Right here? Right now? In the middle of the cafeteria?

God: Yes, right here and now.

Jessica: (To God) But I'll look like a freak or something.

God: But your friend needs your prayers.

Jessica: (To God) I'll pray for her when I get home. Instead of going online tonight, I'll spend time praying. I promise.

God: Well, that would be nice, but that's not enough. She needs you to pray with her now.

Jessica: (To God) Okay, I guess. (To Krista) Umm . . . Krista, can we pray about this? Sometimes when I don't know what to do, the best thing I know to do is pray, and that's how I feel now.

Krista: Okay, I guess.

Jessica and Krista bow their heads. Scene ends.

story today, he had just left Athens and headed to Corinth. Silas and Timothy had brought good news to Paul about the church at Thessalonica (see 1 Thessalonians 3:6) as well as some money from the church at Philippi (see 2 Corinthians 11:9; Philippians 4:4-15). Because Paul received this money, he was able to support himself and devote himself entirely to preaching the gospel.

Continue by stating that Paul experienced opposition from the Jews in Corinth because he was sharing the gospel. The same thing had happened to him previously at a city called Pisidian Antioch (see Acts 13:46-52). However, in both Corinth and Antioch, the Jews' rejection of Paul and his message motivated him to spend more time with non-Jews, or people known as Gentiles. When Paul "shook his garments" (verse 6), he was signifying his frustration with the Jews' opposition as well as declaring freedom from responsibility for them (see Nehemiah 5:13).

Note that an important piece of background information that helps us to better understand the passage is that on both Paul's Galatian and Macedonian journeys, he had begun with a good response from the people only to be forced later to leave them. It is likely that Paul was wondering if this same thing was going to happen in Corinth, a city where he was starting to see some results. Then, one night, God gave Paul a vision and told him to be bold and keep on speaking the gospel. God said that He would be with him and that other believers in the city would support him. As a result of this message from God, Paul stayed in Corinth for 18 months.

Read Acts 18:12-17. Explain that Paul would soon need the strength he received from hearing God's voice, because the Jews attacked him in court. However, just as Paul was beginning to plead his case, Gallio, a Roman leader who had a reputation for being fair, refused to get involved. "If it is a question of words and names and your own law, look to it yourselves," he said (verse 15). Gallio stated that his job was to judge civil and criminal cases, not to help settle religious disputes. This meant that Christianity was not a violation of Roman law. Paul and others had newfound freedom to preach about the gospel.

When you are finished giving this background information, discuss the following questions:

- The vision that God gave to Paul proved to be true. How do you think Paul would have felt standing before Gallio if he hadn't heard from God?
- How do you think he felt appearing before Gallio, confident that he had heard from God?

- How does this relate to the drama we just saw?
- Does Paul act more like a Christian or a non-Christian? Why?

Close the message by sharing that hearing from God can give us all the strength we need just when we need it.

DIG

Option 1: These Drain Me. For this option, you will need copies of "These Drain Me" (found on the next page), pencils, prizes, a whiteboard, a whiteboard pen and a ball. Ahead of time, cut out the cards from the handout.

Divide students into groups of 5 to 8. Explain that at this point we are going to identify a few areas in our lives where we especially need God's strength. Every day we are bombarded with messages that make us feel worthless, useless and weak, so we need God to speak into our lives on a regular basis.

Have the groups come to the front one at a time and choose a card. State that they will have 10 seconds to read the topic listed on the card and come up with the most draining message they can think of about it. These messages can be things they hear from the media, friends or whatever else make them feel weak in these areas. They should be as creative as possible in their answers, as you will be rewarding some of the groups with prizes. It might help your groups if you provide some examples, such as, "Acne makes you ugly," "You need cool clothes or you're a loser" or "It's better to be popular than to be nice."

After the first group picks a card and shares its idea, write it on the whiteboard. State that if we stopped right here and tried to face this message on our own, we would end up feeling pretty depressed. However, the good news is that God has already spoken the truth to us in His Word and has given us strength to face this message.

Hand a ball to the group that has just come up. Have one of the group members throw the ball to another group. The group that catches it has 10 seconds to come up with a response to the energy-draining message. The response needs to sound like something God would say to give us strength. For example, if the draining message was, "You have to have cool clothes to really look good," God's response might be, "True beauty is on the inside, not the outside." Any team that can come up with a relevant Scripture verse (and no, they can't use John 3:16 for every one) will earn a big bonus for their team.

When the group finishes a round, choose a new team to come forward, and then start the process again. Continue this until all the groups have picked up

These Drain Me

The way I look . . .	The number of friends I have . . .
My clothes . . .	My grades . . .
How popular I am at school . . .	How well I do at sports . . .
The stuff I have . . .	How well I do at other activities . . .

and responded to all of the draining message cards. Give prizes to the groups that came up with the most original draining ideas as well as the most biblically accurate and encouraging responses from God.

Option 2: The Addiction. For this option, you will need just this book. Read the following case study to your students:

Ian was an eighth-grader who received a computer last Christmas. His mom got it for him so he could do his homework and do research on the Internet for school projects, but Ian quickly found a whole bunch of other things he could do with it—such as email his friends, visit chat rooms, and even look at pornography sites. At first, Ian would only look at the sites late at night when his mom went to bed. And it wasn't like he looked at them every day—only every two or three days.

However, Ian soon began visiting these sites every night—and sometimes even in the mornings. If his mom was still at work when he came home from school, he would call up his friends and they would come over before dinner and check out the sites as well. They thought Ian was lucky to have a computer in his own bedroom—all their computers were in the family room or in the kitchen.

Over time, Ian felt less and less "lucky." He started to realize that the pornography was controlling him. When his science and health teacher spoke about drug and alcohol addictions, he started to wonder if he might be addicted to porn. So Ian prayed and said, "God, every time I look at porn on the Internet, I'll volunteer to do extra house cleaning chores at home." He thought this would provide the motivation he needed to stop.

But it didn't. Ian kept looking at porn, and—surprise, surprise—his house never got any cleaner.

Now discuss the following questions:

- Do you think Ian was addicted to porn? Why or why not?
- Was Ian relying on God's strength? (*Not really—instead of asking God to help him, he made a bargain with God. Those kinds of bargains don't usually work out so well.*)
- What should Ian have prayed? (*Maybe something like, "God, please help me and strengthen me when I feel tempted."*)

- Was Ian's own strength up to the task of quitting porn? (*No. He needed to seek God, and hopefully even hear from Him, in order to really conquer his temptation.*)
- How would Acts 18:9-10 have encouraged Ian? (*It would have told Ian that God is with him and that there are others around him who can encourage him.*)
- If God can and would give Ian the courage he needs, why does Ian keep failing? (*Because he is relying on his own strength instead of God's. What he needs to do is a combination of praying, reading the Bible and hanging out with other Christians when he needs strength, instead of just trying to make it on his own. He also needs to take the step of speaking to his mom about the problem and get the computer moved out of his room.*)

APPLY

Option 1: Fuel Up. For this option, you will need some kind of toy car. Begin by reminding the group that they have been learning about relying on God and seeking His voice for strength. The question is how we actually do that. What does that mean for our lives tomorrow and the day after? Hold up the toy car and ask the group to think of themselves as being like it. Ask the following questions:

- If we drive around all day, what will eventually happen to us? (*We'll run out of gas.*)
- What should we do to get more fuel? (*Go to a gas station.*)

Explain that the problem is that many times we are driving around but we never stop at a gas station. We might even be yelling to God, "Hey, fill me up with some strength here," but we never stop to actually be filled.

Ask the students if they would be willing to make a commitment to spend seven minutes a day being refilled by God this week. Why seven minutes? Well, seven minutes is about as long as two television commercials run. Can we really say we love God if we can't give Him two commercials? In seven minutes, we can not only read a small portion of the Bible, but we can also spend some time praying about the things that are important to us and the areas where we need God's strength.

Ask the group members to raise their hands if they would be willing to give God seven minutes a day so they can hear from Him and be refilled by Him.

Close in prayer, asking God to help them hear His voice so that they can get the strength they need.

Option 2: Strong Songs. For this option, you will need some worship music (especially songs that relate to God's strength and power) and a way to play it for your group.

Explain to the group that if we look carefully at what God said to Paul and why He said it, we can see that it relates to Paul's need for courage. We all encounter things that scare us, such as losing our friends, or our parents getting a divorce, or failing a test, or not getting into the college we want. Ask the students to think about one thing that is scaring them right now. State that you are going to play some worship music, and as the song plays they need to let the words speak to them and give them courage. When someone feels that he or she has received courage from God, he or she can stand up and keep singing.

Once several students have stood up (or your time is almost over), ask everyone to be seated. Explain that worship music is a great way to hear from God and be strengthened. Challenge the students to choose one worship song that is their favorite. Any time this week they feel afraid or unsure of themselves, they can think about that song (and maybe even sing it in their heads or out loud). They will be surprised at how much more strength they will have as God speaks to them.

Conclude by thanking God in prayer for the way He gives us courage. Ask Him to make you and the group aware of His voice this week.

REFLECT

The following short devotions are for the students to reflect on and answer during the week. You can make a copy of these pages and distribute to your class or download and print from **www.gospellight.com/uncommon/jh_listening_to_God.zip.**

1—ONWARD, CHRISTIAN SOLDIER

How much do you know about soldiers? Take the following true/false test to find out.

Women aren't allowed to be soldiers.	True	False
A soldier must put others before himself or herself.	True	False

The smartest thing a soldier can do when facing an enemy is run for the hills and hide.	True	False
A deserter is a soldier who loves chocolate cake.	True	False
A soldier needs to be brave and determined.	True	False

Good soldiers are willing to face their enemies even when they are scared. They are part of a team that works together to win a victory. That team has a leader who needs to be wise and know how to help the soldiers fight well. The soldiers must listen to the leader and follow the commands given to them.

Hmm . . . that's the kind of Christian soldier that Jesus, our leader, wants us to be. He is with us every step of the way, and He knows how to win the victory. He also knows what it is like to face scary things, and when you listen to His voice, you will gain strength. He will fight beside you and never leave you.

Right now, what or who is your greatest fear?

_____

_____

_____

What do you think "winning the victory" means in your life?

_____

_____

_____

2—A REAL PEST

Hey, quit bugging me and go read Luke 18:1-8.

If you are the owner of a cat, you know about persistence. When a cat decides it is time for breakfast, it will leap on your bed and walk on your stomach. If you don't respond, it will begin yowling. At that point, you might as well get up, because this persistent creature won't quit bugging you until you feed it.

Jesus said that we need to be like this when we talk to God. In Luke 18:1-8, He told a story known as the Parable of the Persistent Widow. In this parable, a woman keeps bothering a judge to get justice. How does the judge respond to himself?

- ❑ *She is right, and I need to do something about it.*
- ❑ *She is right, but there's nothing I can do for her.*

- ❏   *I am going to pretend I didn't hear her.*
- ❏   *I don't really care, but if I don't do something she'll just be back here again tomorrow.*
- ❏   *This woman is a real pest, and I'm going to tell her to leave me alone.*

Do you think it is odd the judge responded this way? How would you have answered the woman?

_____

_____

_____

What does Jesus go on to say that God will do for those who seek Him?

_____

_____

_____

You need persistence when it comes to following Jesus. It is remarkable how many obstacles will suddenly appear when you begin to do something God has told you to do. However, when you ask for God's help and are persistent—like the woman in the story—you will break through and succeed.

3—A DIFFERENT VIEWPOINT

Dying is a pretty scary subject for most people, but the apostle Paul had a different view. As one who regularly heard from God, he had a different viewpoint of life on this earth. Read the following verses, and then write down what Paul said about death:

Philippians 1:21

_____

_____

_____

Romans 8:38-39

_____

_____

_____

Romans 8:11

_____

_____

_____

Of course, this didn't mean that Paul took up extreme sports or did other dangerous things to hurry up his arrival into heaven (and neither should you). He cared deeply about the people in his life and didn't want to leave them (see Philippians 1:24). It just means that Paul was so focused on doing what God had told him to do—sharing the good news about Jesus to others—that he didn't fear what anyone would do to him.

4—WHAT CAN I DO?

John Wooden, one of the greatest basketball coaches of all time, once said, "Do not let what you cannot do interfere with what you can do." What do you think this means?

_____

_____

_____

_____

This is actually good advice: Don't miss out on life because you are spending your time being upset about what you do not know how to do! In 1 Timothy 4:12, Paul gave a young pastor this same advice. He told Timothy not to let anyone look down on him because he was young. What did Paul instruct Timothy to do instead?

- ❏ Get even with those doubters.
- ❏ Ignore them.
- ❏ Set an example for them.
- ❏ Be humble and admit that they are probably right.

God spoke words of *strength* through the apostle Paul to Timothy. Is there something that you feel you should be doing in your life right now that you are *not* doing because you don't know how? If so, say a prayer today asking God for strength and to help you accomplish that thing.

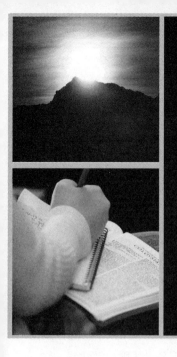

SEEKING GOD'S VOICE FOR TRANSFORMATION

THE BIG IDEA

When we seek God's voice, He often tells us to do tough things in order to bring transformation in our lives.

THE BIGGEST VERSE

"And now, compelled by the Spirit, I am going to Jerusalem, not knowing what will happen to me there. . . . I consider my life worth nothing to me; my only aim is to finish the race and complete the task the Lord Jesus has given me—the task of testifying to the good news of God's grace" (Acts 20:22,24).

LESSON AIMS

In this session, you will guide students to (1) realize that doing what God wants them to do is more important than their own comfort; (2) feel encouraged that God is not only working through them but also in them; and (3) view hard things as opportunities to grow closer to God.

OTHER IMPORTANT VERSES

Judges 6:11; Esther 2:17; Isaiah 6:8,11; Amos 7:14; Matthew 9:9; Mark 1:16; Acts 9:1-2; 20:13-24; Romans 12:2; 2 Corinthians 1:5-6; Philippians 3:4-7

Note: Additional options and worksheets in 8¹/₂" x 11" format for this session are available for download at **www.gospellight.com/uncommon/jh_listening_to_God.zip**.

STARTER

Option 1: The Tough Stuff. For this option, you will need some index cards, a hat and pencils.

Greet students and distribute an index card and a pencil to each person. Once they have their cards, explain that they need to write down the toughest thing they can imagine having to do this week. It can be anything from eating a caterpillar to telling the entire school the name of the girl/boy on whom they have a crush. They will have 30 seconds to come up with an idea and write it down on the card. Start the timer.

When 30 seconds is up, collect the cards and place them in a hat. Explain that you will be pulling two cards out of the hat. If students feel that the first card you read is the toughest thing, they should move to the left side of the room. If they feel that the second card you read is tougher, they should move to the right side of the room. At this point, you might want to ask a couple of the students to share why they chose the option they did. Repeat this exercise until all the cards are gone.

Afterward, lead the group in the following discussion:

- Out of all the cards I read to you, which one did you think was the toughest? Why?
- Who are the people in your life who make you do tougher things: your parents or your friends?
- What about God? Does He make you do tough things?
- Why do you think that God would make you do something really tough?

Explain that God does call us to do some tough things. Once we hear His voice and understand that He has called us to do something really hard, we have a choice. We can refuse, or we can do it. Today, we will be discussing how if we agree to do what God has asked—no matter how hard it is—there is generally something good in it for us.

Option 2: Difficult Scavenger Hunt. For this option, you will need prizes, adult volunteers and several cell phones for the adult leaders. Ahead of time, plan a scavenger hunt that fits your meeting place. Ideally, there should be six to eight items, each located in a different part of the church, that are somewhat difficult to find. You will need to think of a hint for each item that is hard, but not impossible to figure out. Make sure each adult volunteer has a cell phone and your hint list. Write down that person's cell phone number to give to one of the teams.

You might want to come up with a theme for your scavenger hunt, such as "life at school" or "fast-food frenzy." If you choose "fast-food frenzy," you will need to come up with six to eight fast-food items and hide them in different locations around the church building. When a team finds the hamburger or the milkshake, they must eat or drink it to be able to call a certain number on the cell phone and get the next clue. Each phone will have one of your adult volunteers on the other end giving the next hint. In addition, you might want to start your teams with different initial clues and mix up the order of subsequent clues so that they don't just follow each other around from station to station.

Greet students and divide them into as many teams as you have cell phones (ideally, no more than 10 students per team). Give each team the number of the cell phone they will be calling for hints. Explain the scavenger hunt rules to the students and make sure they understand that they need to pay attention to the clue when they call in to get it. They cannot ask the person to repeat it on the same phone call, but they can call back and ask for it again. The problem with calling back, though, is that it wastes valuable time. The team that finds the most items wins the game.

After the scavenger hunt, congratulate the winning team and give them the prizes. Then discuss the following questions:

- On a scale of 1 to 5, with 1 being super easy and 5 being very hard, what number would you give this scavenger hunt?
- Think about the things God has asked you to do. On a scale of 1 to 5, how hard are those things?

The truth is that God often calls us to do some things that are extremely challenging. However, as we will see today, no matter how tough they are, we will be blessed if we do them.

Youth Leader Tip

While you want students to feel like the group is theirs, you want to be near them as they make decisions. Don't be afraid to send an adult into a small group to guide discussion and ensure that everyone is being heard.

MESSAGE

Option 1: Toughest Goodbye. For this option, you will need a Bible, the movie *Armageddon* and some way to show it to your group. Ahead of time, find the scene in the movie where Harry (played by Bruce Willis) has to say goodbye to his daughter, Grace (played by Liv Tyler), knowing that he will never see her again. Have this scene ready to play before the meeting.

Begin by asking the students the following questions:

- In what languages can you say "goodbye"?
- What's the toughest goodbye you have ever had to say?
- What made it so tough?

State that saying goodbye is often tough, especially if it is to someone we really care about or if we know it is going to be a long time before we see that person again. Tell the group that you are going to show them a scene from the movie *Armageddon.* Do a brief summary of what has happened in the movie up to this point. A large asteroid is plummeting toward the earth, so NASA sends up a team of workers to drill a hole into the center of the asteroid and place a nuclear bomb there. The theory is that when the bomb explodes, it will break up the asteroid into smaller pieces and will no longer threaten Earth. However, the plan changes when the workers realize one of them will have to stay behind and manually detonate the bomb. A.J. (played by Ben Affleck) draws the straw that indicates he will be the one to stay. A.J. is dating a woman named Grace, who is Harry's daughter. Harry tricks A.J. and forces him to go back home to be with Grace. Harry explodes the asteroid and dies in the process.

Continue by stating that the scene they are about to watch depicts the emotional goodbye between Harry and his daughter. Play the scene. When it is finished, explain that Harry had to say goodbye to his daughter, someone he cared deeply about. His daughter was the most important person in the world to him, and he knew that he would never see her again. In the same way, the apostle Paul had to say goodbye to the leaders of the church at Ephesus, whom he cared for deeply. There was no asteroid involved, but Paul knew that he would not see them again, and the parting was painful.

Read Acts 20:17-24. Explain that this was Paul's goodbye speech to the Ephesians. Paul had faced opposition in that city, so he began by telling them what he had done among them as a dedicated servant and messenger of Christ. Paul went on to share his plans to go to Jerusalem. He told the Ephesians that he was "compelled by the Spirit" to go there (verse 22), though he didn't know what would happen to him once he got there.[1] Paul wanted to share the gospel in that region and take money that had been donated from other cities to help the non-Jews living there. Now discuss the following questions:

- What kinds of things would have been important for Paul to say to the Ephesians, as he knew he might not see them again? (*As it says in verse 21, Paul preached about their need to repent and have faith in Christ.*)
- What do you think it means to be "compelled by the Spirit"? (*It means to know that God was sending him there. Paul had heard God's voice and was obeying His will.*)
- What is Paul's primary goal? (*To finish the race and complete the task that Jesus had given to him.*)
- How is this goal connected to hearing God's voice? (*Paul knew that the more he obeyed God—even if he didn't know the final outcome—the more his attitude would be changed to embrace what God had given him to do.*)
- Up to this time, Paul had been an important and prominent leader. Why would he say that his life meant nothing to him? (*Because he knew that in comparison to the value of obeying God, his life was worthless.*)

Read Acts 21:4 and 12 aloud. State that several well-meaning people in the cities Paul visited on his way to Jerusalem tried to stop him from going there. For Paul, it must have seemed that he was receiving two messages that didn't agree with each other: (1) the Holy Spirit was telling him to go to Jerusalem, but (2) his friends—who had wisdom—were urging him not to go. Ask the group which of these two Paul ultimately followed. In the end, Paul went against what his friends and co-workers were telling him because he knew that obeying God was more important than listening to the wise people around him. After all, God is much wiser than anybody else!

Read Acts 21:13-14. Point out that Paul's friends didn't want him to go, but they eventually realized that Paul had heard from God in this matter. Ask if any of them have ever been in a similar situation where their friends or family advised them to do one thing, but they felt God was calling them to do something else.

Option 2: On to Jerusalem. For this option, you will need a Bible, a squirt gun, a sign that says "Jerusalem," some tape and five volunteers. Ahead of time, tape your Jerusalem sign to a wall in your meeting room. Ask the five volunteers to do the following during the meeting:

- Two of them will be your "blockers." The blockers should be hiding behind a door or a couch. When you send the Paul actor to Jerusalem (the Jerusalem sign) in part one of the message, the blockers will jump up and try to block the sign from his view.

- One of the volunteers will be "the attacker." He or she should have a squirt gun. The attacker should be hiding until you begin to talk about Paul facing possible pain and suffering once he reaches Jerusalem in part two of the message. At this point, the attacker will jump up and begin to squirt your Paul actor with his water gun.

- The remaining two volunteers are "the discouragers." They should be hiding until you begin to talk about well-meaning people who tried to discourage Paul in part three of the message. At this point, they should jump up, grab Paul's arm and try to discourage him by saying, "It's too dangerous!" "We need you here!" and "Who will take care of your cat when you leave?"

Introduce this talk by setting the stage for Paul's goodbye speech to the Ephesian elders. Point out that Paul began his speech by reminding these friends about how he had shared the gospel with them and served among them faithfully. He then went on to say that he felt God was telling him to go to Jerusalem, though he didn't know what would happen to him once he got there. Paul wanted to share the gospel in that region and take money that had been donated from other cities to help the Gentiles (non-Jews) living there.

Read Paul's words in Acts 20:22-24. Choose a student to play the part of "Paul," and have him or her come to the front of the room. Explain that obeying God's voice can sometimes be hard. One reason is because *it often takes us to unknown places.* Send your "Paul" toward the Jerusalem sign. State that Paul is leaving for Jerusalem. At this point, the blockers will get in front of the Jerusalem sign and hide it from Paul. Explain that Paul knew where he was supposed to go, but didn't know exactly what would happen once he got there.

Continue by stating that a second reason why obeying God's voice can be hard is because *it often involves doing something painful.* Reread Acts 20:23, pointing out the bleak circumstances that would probably meet Paul once he got to Jerusalem. At this point, your student with the water gun should pop up and begin to squirt "Paul." Explain that the worst that can happen to the Paul they see here today is that he will get wet, but the Paul in the Bible could be facing beatings, imprisonment and even death.

State that a third reason why obeying God's voice can be hard is because *others may discourage us.* Read Acts 21:4 and 12. Explain that there were some well-meaning people in the cities Paul visited on his way to Jerusalem who tried to stop him from doing what God had told him to do. At this point, the discouragers should appear, begin to pull your Paul actor away from the Jerusalem sign, and tell him all of the reasons why he should not go to Jerusalem. Have all the actors sit down.

Read Acts 21:13-14 aloud. Explain that the people's willingness to trust Paul's understanding of God's will (even when they themselves didn't) shows how much they respected Paul. Conclude by asking the students why they think we should do what God tells us to do if we know we might face fear, pain and discouragement. Read Acts 20:24 and explain that Paul knew that nothing was as important as obeying God. The more he followed God's voice, the more God was with him and worked through him. Paul grew in his faith and became willing to pursue God's goals instead of his own.

DIG

Option 1: Nicely Toasted. For this option, you will need some bread and a toaster. Ahead of time, place a sign near the toaster that says, "Doing God's will." Also, make sure you place the toaster close to an electrical outlet so you can actually plug it in.

Explain that the toaster represents doing God's will and the bread represents us. Let's say God asks us to do something, and we say yes. We are like the toast that goes into the toaster. Ask the group what they think are some of the things God wants us to do. Let your students come up with ideas as you put the bread into the toaster and start it. Challenge them to not stop sharing ideas until the bread is finished being toasted.

When the bread pops up, hold it up and ask the group members how the bread has changed. (The answer would be that the bread is now golden

<u>Youth Leader Tip</u>
Whenever you can, plan surprises into your meetings. The more your students are shocked and amazed by what happens, the more they will remember it (and, hopefully, the more they will act on it!).

brown—or blackened, depending on your particular taste.) Explain that when we do what God wants us to do, He makes us different as well. He changes us and helps us to have more of His attitude and perspective.

Option 2: To Go or Not to Go. For this option, you will need two adults and copies of "To Go or Not to Go" (found on the following page). Ahead of time, assign at least one adult to each debate position on the handout. Ask the adult leaders to be ready to debate the arguments listed under their positions, as well as anything else they can think of, in front of the students during the meeting. Begin by reading the following story to the group members:

Bradley was a seventh-grader who thought things were going pretty well for him. Although he wasn't the most popular kid at his school, he had friends who seemed to like him. His family was pretty cool and didn't embarrass him too much. He liked his youth group and was learning to play guitar so he could help out on the music worship team.

Toward the end of Bradley's seventh-grade year, his parents approached him and his little sister with the idea of being missionaries to Argentina. "What?" he said, "You're going to leave me here?"

His mom answered, "No, actually, you would be coming with us."

"No way," Bradley said. "I don't want to leave my friends and the youth group. This stinks."

No matter how much Bradley argued, his parents were convinced that God's will was for them to go to Argentina. Nine months later, after they had raised the financial support they needed, Bradley said goodbye to his friends and boarded the plane.

Argentina was even worse than Bradley expected. The other kids at his school couldn't speak English well, and Bradley's Spanish was even worse, so they couldn't talk to each other. The members of the church with whom his parents were supposed to be involved got into a big fight the month they arrived and eventually split up. To top it all off, his mom caught some weird disease and ended up spending most days in bed. His dad spent most of his time taking care of his mom and left Bradley and his sister to fend for themselves.

After living in Argentina for 11 months, Bradley's parents decided that it was better to be in America so his mom could get the medical care she needed. As they were packing up their things, Bradley told his dad, "See, this wasn't God's will after all."

TO GO OR NOT TO GO

Bradley is right about Argentina not being God's will because . . .	Bradley is wrong about Argentina not being God's will because . . .
God protects people who obey Him. His mom wouldn't have gotten sick if his family was really hearing from God.	God doesn't guarantee total protection against things in this life. He grants eternal life.
God brings happiness to those who hear His voice and obey it.	God brings something deeper than happiness—He brings joy and contentment.
If we face closed doors, like at that church in Argentina, it can't be God's will.	Closed doors may not be the end of the story, for God often wants us to work harder to open the doors, or trust Him to open doors in His timing.
God works through people who are hearing His voice and obeying Him. Nothing happened through Bradley's family.	God not only works through people but also in them to make them more like Christ.

Ask the students to raise their hands if they agree with Bradley when he said that it wasn't God's will for the family to go to Argentina. Then ask for those who disagree to raise their hands. Next, introduce the adults who have prepared for the debate. Let them discuss the various points supporting and disagreeing with Bradley's position. Explain to the group members that they are welcome to share any thoughts or ideas when they think of them. When the adults finish the debate, ask the group the following questions:

- So, was it God's will or not for Bradley's family to go to Argentina?
- Who has changed your mind since I first asked that question?
- Which arguments convinced you?
- What do you think God was trying to teach Bradley?
- How about his parents?

Explain that as Paul understood, hearing from God and doing His will doesn't mean our lives will be one big happy walk down a rosy path. Hard things such as disease, loneliness and rejection will happen, but if we're open to God, we will find that He can work *in* us and show us new things about what it means to follow Him.

APPLY

Option 1: I've Got It Together . . . Not! For this option, you will need two female students who will be your actors and copies of the "I've Got It Together . . . Not!" drama (found on the next two pages). Ahead of time, meet with your actors, give them copies of the script and assign the parts of Bianca and Amy. Have them practice so they will be ready to perform the drama during the meeting.

Explain to the group members that many times when we go through hard things, we think we can't share them with others, especially non-Christians. We're afraid that if we do, it will somehow make God look bad, because our lives are supposed to be perfect if we follow Him. So we act a lot like what we will see in the following drama. Have the students act out scene one.

When the scene is finished, explain that Paul should be our example. He admitted his problems to others. We can do the same. Have the students act out scene two. When they are finished, ask the group how the two scenes were different. Which performance showed us a better witness for Christ? (The answer would be scene two.) State that the truth is that we do not need Jesus just once when we ask Him to take over our lives and be our Savior. We need

The Cast
Bianca
Amy

The Props
Some schoolbooks

Scene One

The scene opens with Bianca and Amy walking together at school carrying schoolbooks.

Bianca: Amy, I'm glad to finally get the chance to talk to you. Last night when you called you sounded so upset about your parents fighting. How are you?

Amy: I'm fine.

Bianca: Well, what happened with your parents?

Amy: They kept fighting. It was so loud that I had to put the pillow over my head to fall asleep. And when I woke up, my dad's car was gone. I don't even think he slept at home last night.

Bianca: So, how's your mom?

Amy: She's fine. Well, enough about my family and me. (In a fake, cheerful and upbeat voice) How are you?

Bianca: Well, I'm doing pretty well, except for being way behind on my science fair project. But I'm mostly concerned about you. Are you sure you're okay?

Amy: (Still way too cheerful) Yes, I got up early and read my Bible as I was drying my hair. It helped, and everything is good now.

Bianca: Good, I'm glad.

Amy: Yeah, it's really not a problem. God makes my life pretty perfect.

Bianca: (In a disbelieving and skeptical tone of voice) Yeah, sure . . .

Scene Two

The scene opens with Bianca and Amy walking together at school carrying schoolbooks.

Bianca: Amy, I'm glad to finally get the chance to talk to you. Last night when you called you sounded so upset about your parents fighting. How are you?

Amy: Not so good. My parents fought so late last night that I had to finally put the pillow over my head to fall asleep. And my dad's car was gone this morning, so I think he spent the night somewhere else.

Bianca: Wow, I'm really sorry.

Amy: Me too. My mom is still really upset. Her eyes were all red and puffy this morning when she handed me lunch money, so I know she was crying a lot.

Bianca: So how about you . . . are you okay?

Amy: I guess so. I'm pretty scared, but I read a little bit in the Bible this morning, and it kind of helped.

Bianca: Really? What did it say?

Amy: Well, I read some stuff in Psalm 27:10 about God never leaving me, which makes me feel better. I mean, not all better or anything, but at least a little better. I'm looking forward to going to church tomorrow. Whenever I'm down, being there and thinking about God helps.

Bianca: That's good.

Amy: I know your parents aren't fighting or anything, but I know you're pretty scared about your brother's drinking. Do you think you would like to come to church with me?

Bianca: Maybe. Ask me again tomorrow.

Amy: I sure will.

Him *every day*, and others need to know that we need Him every day. Close in prayer, giving the group members some quiet time on their own to pray about the tough things they are experiencing.

Option 2: Bubble Gum. For this option, you will need some bubble gum, index cards and pencils.

Distribute the index cards and pencils and ask the students to write down the hardest thing they're going through right now (make sure it is something they are willing to share). Collect the cards and read each aloud. After each card, ask the group members how what you have just read might be something God is using to help the person grow closer to Him.

Hold up a piece of bubble gum. Put it in your mouth and explain that right now the gum is hard and tough to chew. However, once you start to chew it, it changes and becomes softer. The same thing is true for us. No, God doesn't chew us, but the things He asks us to do give us opportunities for Him to soften our hearts and become open to hearing even more from Him in the future. Distribute the bubble gum and close in prayer, thanking God for the ways He changes us through the hard things in our lives.

REFLECT

The following short devotions are for the students to reflect on and answer during the week. You can make a copy of these pages and distribute to your class or download and print from **www.gospellight.com/uncommon/jh_listening_to_God.zip**.

1—UNCOMFORTABLE

Nobody likes to feel uncomforatable, but does it sometimes have a purpose? Read 2 Corinthians 1:5-6 to find out.

A mother bald eagle may lay two or three eggs in a huge nest that is eight feet across. Most of the nest is made of sticks, but it is also carefully lined with soft materials so that when the baby birds hatch, they will have a soft surface on which to rest. The eaglets (yes, that's what they're called) grow quickly, and soon the nest becomes too small for them. It becomes uncomfortable. So they begin to do something called "fledging" or "branching"—they hop from the nest to the branches of the tree and then back to the nest. This is how they get ready to begin flying.

Finally, the day arrives when the eaglets have to leave the nest. To do this, they have to leap off the branch and launch into the air. It sounds scary, but they will never fly if they don't do this.

When the Holy Spirit begins to talk to you about something He wants you to work on or change, it probably won't be comfortable for you. You might like what you are doing and don't want to change. However, God knows that you need to change, so He will continue to prepare you for it (and sometimes even make you get out of the nest!).

Read 2 Corinthians 1:6. What do "sufferings" (uncomfortable situations) bring?

_____

_____

_____

Is there anything you are doing in your life right now that you feel God is asking you to change? If so, what are you doing about it?

_____

_____

_____

_____

Don't be afraid. When God asks you to change something, the Holy Spirit will be right there with you to see you through. He won't let you fall.

2—MAKE ME AN INSTRUMENT

When you hear God calling, what do you do? Read Isaiah 6:8 to find out how one person in the Bible responded.

Francesco Bernadone, also known as Francis of Assisi, had the right attitude when it came to following God's voice. Read the following prayer that he wrote about change, and circle all of the opposites you find (for example, "hatred"/"love").

Lord, make me an instrument of your Peace.
Where there is hatred, let me sow love.
Where there is injury, pardon.
Where there is doubt, faith.

Where there is despair, hope.
Where there is darkness, light.
Where there is sadness, joy!

Look at Isaiah 6:8. We previously looked at how Jonah responded when God called him to do something—he ran away. But Isaiah made a different choice. What did he say?

_____

_____

_____

Now look at Isaiah 6:11. How long was Isaiah to do what God asked him to do?

_____

_____

_____

Do you think this would have been easy for Isaiah? Why or why not?

_____

_____

_____

Following God's voice isn't always easy, but it's always much better for us in the long run!

3—NIGHT AND DAY

There were many people in the Bible whose lives changed radically—like night and day. See if you can match the following biblical characters with what they used to do before God called them to follow Him. (If you need help, look up the following verses: Judges 6:11; Esther 2:17; Amos 7:14; Matthew 9:9; Mark 1:16; Acts 9:1-2.)

Paul	a queen
Gideon	a tax collector
Esther	a fisherman
Amos	a Christian-killer
Matthew	a shepherd and gardener
Andrew	a wheat farmer

Choose one of the people on the list. Do you think it was hard for this person to change? Why or why not?

_____

_____

_____

Read Philippians 3:4-7. What does Paul say about his life before he met Christ?

_____

_____

_____

Notice in the above list that God did not move Esther out of her role as queen. However, because she was willing to do what God asked, He used her right where she was—and saved the Israelites in the process! God can also use you right where you are today if you are willing to follow His voice.

4—JUST DO IT!

Looking for some real change? Turn to Romans 12:2.

When you were younger, perhaps you argued with your parents about something they wanted you to change. Which of the following did they get after you the most about?

- ❏ Clean up your room!
- ❏ Do your homework!
- ❏ Turn off the TV and go outside!
- ❏ No snacks before dinner!

Maybe you went along with your parents just to get them off your back, but you didn't really change anything you were doing. What does Paul say about real change in Romans 12:2?

Be _____ by the _____ of your _____.

Real change happens when you make a decision to do what God says and allow Him to change your behavior. Over time, as you learn to trust in Him, He will take you to the next level and bring lasting change in your life! Today, say a prayer thanking God for loving you and helping you to become what He wants you to be.

SEEKING GOD'S VOICE IN SHARING THE GOSPEL

THE BIG IDEA

Seeking God's voice gives us the courage we need to share the gospel.

THE BIGGEST VERSE

"The Lord stood near Paul and said, 'Take courage! As you have testified about me in Jerusalem, so you must also testify in Rome'" (Acts 23:11).

SESSION AIMS

In this lesson you will guide students to (1) recognize that though sharing their faith may take more time and effort than they expected, God will open doors for them to tell others about Jesus; (2) feel motivated to share with people, knowing that God has already called them to do so; (3) identify the people they will have a chance to share with this week, pray for them and reach out to them.

OTHER IMPORTANT VERSES

Matthew 5:13-16; 10:14-16; 28:18-20; Mark 1:16-18; Luke 15:1-7; 19:10; John 4:35-37; 17:18; Acts 23:11,34-35; 24:25-26; 27:6-8,13-18,39-41; 28:1-6,17-31; 1 Corinthians 3:5-8

Note: Additional options and worksheets in 8¹/₂" x 11" format for this session are available for download at **www.gospellight.com/uncommon/jh_listening_to_God.zip**.

STARTER

Option 1: Spread the Good News. For this option, you will need one adult volunteer and some donuts (or other food) that you keep outside of your room. Ahead of time, have the adult volunteer go outside the room to be in charge of the donuts. Instruct the volunteer to tell the group members that they have to eat the donut inside the room and then let them have a donut.

Greet the students and let them know that they can talk and hang out for a few minutes. Tell a few of the students about the free donuts right outside of your room and have them spread the word. Let them know that there are enough donuts for everyone. Your adult volunteer will give the students instructions and then a donut.

See how long it takes before every student either hears the message or sees others walking back into the room holding their donuts. When everyone has a treat, call the group back together and lead them in the following discussion:

- I only told two people about the food. How did the word get out so fast?
- What kind of news are we likely to share quickly? (*Good news!*)
- What made you want to share this good news? (*You probably wanted your friends to have some food, especially since you knew there was enough for everybody.*)
- When is it tough to share good news with others? (*Most likely when you are afraid that it will not seem as good to them as it does to you, or you're afraid your friends will think you are dorky for telling them.*)

Explain that when we hear good news—and really believe it's good news—we are more likely to share it with others. Even if we don't share it verbally, others will be able to see something different about us (in this case, the fact that the group members were holding donuts or still had some powdered sugar stuck to their mouths) and will want to experience the good news as well.

Conclude by stating that sometimes it is hard or even scary for us to share with others. However, hearing God's voice will give us the courage and strength we need to get past anything that might keep us silent.

Option 2: Share Your Clothespins. For this option, you will need several spring-type clothespins (at least two per student).

Greet the group members and give each two clothespins. When you say the word "go," they are to try to clip the clothespins on everyone else's clothing. The winners are the students who have no pins on them or in their hands when you yell "stop."

After a few rounds, have everyone grab a seat. State how amazed you are at how quickly each person was willing to share what he or she had with the rest of the group. Explain that when it comes to sharing about Jesus, sometimes we don't want to do it right away—often because we are afraid to do so for some reason. However, as we will learn in today's message, hearing God's voice will fill us with courage and determination to share with others, no matter what.

MESSAGE

Option 1: The Tale of Pablo. For this option, you will need copies of the drama "The Tale of Pablo" (found on the next page) and some Bibles.

Choose 12 volunteers to perform the actions and lines of the various characters in the "The Tale of Pablo." You will be reading the part of the narrator. If any of the actors do a half-hearted job, make that person do his or her action or line again. If you have fewer than 12 students, give your students multiple roles (which in many ways makes this drama even more amusing).

When the drama is finished, applaud and congratulate these sure-to-win-an-Oscar performers. Explain that if any of the group members guessed that Pablo was actually Paul from the Bible, they were right. Paul had been arrested for sharing about Jesus, because this was a message the Jews found offensive, and therefore they used it as grounds for his arrest and prosecution. Explain that Paul never tried to go to Washington, DC, like in the "Tale of Pablo," but God told him to go to Rome. It took him several court appearances, a shipwreck and many years, but he finally made it there just as God said he would.

Read Acts 28:17-31. Explain that Paul did ultimately receive his chance to share the gospel with the Jewish leaders. Some of the leaders agreed with him, but others decided he was wrong. In addition, during the next two years while Paul was awaiting his final trial in Rome, God fulfilled His original promise by having Paul share the gospel in Rome.[1]

Option 2: Taking Steps. For this option, you will need a flower, some seeds, and a Bible. Begin by explaining that Paul was pretty good at hearing God's voice and doing what the Lord told him to do. In today's episode of "The Adventures in Paul," we find Paul once again hearing from God.

Read Acts 23:11. State that though Paul had this promise, he also had many delays in getting to Rome. Here are a few of them:

- Paul had to stay in prison to wait for the Jews who brought charges against him to arrive (Acts 23:34-35).

The Tale of Pablo

Cast of Characters

Pablo	A guard
God	A judge
A bed	A desk
Three bad guys	Storm cloud
A horse	An island

One night, Pablo, the hero of our story, lay asleep on a bed in prison. He was tossing, turning and snoring loudly. Suddenly he awoke and sat up straight. He heard God say in a loud and powerful voice, "Hey, Pablo, don't be scared. You have told others about me in your town. Now you are going to share about me in Washington, DC."

Meanwhile, three bad guys were huddled together nearby. They hated Pablo. They made an agreement to kill Pablo. They rubbed their hands together in delight at the prospect of getting rid of Pablo. However, when the prison guard heard about the plot to kill Pablo, he ordered Pablo to be transferred on a horse to another prison. The horse got a little confused, though, and walked around the stage two times with Pablo on his back. Finally, they made it to the other prison.

Later on, a guard took Pablo before the judge. Pablo told the judge, "I want to go to Washington, DC, and present my case." The judge slapped his desk and said, "It shall be done."

Pablo and a prison guard hopped over and got on board a boat headed to DC (yes, we mean literally hopped). Soon a storm cloud came right near them and blew on them. The cloud kept blowing and blowing and blowing. It was blowing so hard that eventually Pablo and the prison guard ended up overboard and had to swim for the shore.

The guard swam freestyle, but Pablo swam the dog paddle. Pablo even panted like a dog. When they finally reached an island, they collapsed onto the sand and moaned, "Yea, we made it." Finally, they found another boat and set sail for DC. When they got close to DC, Pablo was so excited that he started to sing "The Star-Spangled Banner" at the top of his lungs. The prison guard covered his ears and kept yelling, "Make it stop, make it stop," but everyone who heard Pablo clapped wildly for him.

- Felix, the Roman governor in Caesarea, was hoping Paul would offer him a bribe, so he kept him in jail for two years (Acts 24:25-26).
- The wind was wimpy and worked against Paul when he was on a ship headed for Rome (Acts 27:6-8).
- A storm came and wrecked the ship that Paul was on so badly that they had to run it aground on an unknown island (Acts 27:13-18,39-41).
- Paul was bitten by a snake on this island, but suffered no effects from it (Acts 28:1-6).

Explain that based on all these events, one would think Paul would have given up on ever getting to Rome. But, surprise, surprise, God is faithful. Paul did make it to Rome and proclaimed the gospel there for two years.

Share an experience from your past of when you felt burdened to share the gospel with a friend, but when you did, it seemed to take forever for that person to respond. Sometimes, people just don't accept Jesus into their lives as quickly as we would like! At times like these, we need to remember two things that must have certainly helped Paul. First, *it's ultimately God's work.* Hold up the flower and the seeds. Have the group members imagine that the flower came from their garden. They were the ones who planted the seed and watered it. However, they did not make it grow. God did. The same is true when it comes to seeing people come to know Christ. Paul understood this and explained it to the people in Corinth. In 1 Corinthians 3:5-8 he wrote that it is God who makes things grow, not us. Those who accept Christ and grow in their faith are ultimately responding to God's work, not ours.

State that a second point that would have helped Paul is that when a person receives Christ is *ultimately up to God's timing.* Choose a volunteer to come forward. Point that person toward a door or wall, making sure he or she is standing five steps away from it. Explain that the volunteer represents a non-Christian and that door/wall is salvation. Let's say we share about how we became Christians. The person hears the gospel for the first time, and it brings him or her one step closer to the door. (Have the volunteer take a step closer to the door or wall.)

Continue by stating that at this point we can't really see much progress, but we decide to invite that person to church anyway. That person says yes, comes, and is touched by the worship music. He or she takes another step forward. (The volunteer should take another step.) Once again, we might not realize that the person is moving forward, but he or she is. Then we tell the person that we will be praying for his or her sick grandma, and the person is so touched that he or she takes another step. (Have the volunteer take another step.) Each time we share a little bit of our faith, the person is given the chance to walk closer to salvation. One day, he or she might take the final step toward becoming a Christian. (The volunteer should now take the final step.)

Ask the group which step they think was the most important. The truth is that they are all equally important, because each one brought that person closer. We may never know how much we're impacting our friends and helping them to get closer to God, but if we add up all the little steps, they equal one big leap toward God.

DIG

Option 1: Two Calls. For this option, you will need two cell phones and a megaphone. (If you can't obtain a megaphone, just make one by rolling up a large sheet of paper into the shape of a cone.) Ahead of time, give one cell phone to an adult leader or student to keep hidden in a pocket or purse. Keep the other cell phone for yourself.

Explain to the group that when we hear stories from the Bible like the one about Paul, sometimes we think, *Sure, that's great for Paul. He knew exactly what God wanted him to do and where God wanted him to go. But I haven't seen God in any visions or heard Him speak out loud to me. How do I know what I'm supposed to do?*

State that there are two ways God speaks to us. The first way is a specific calling, meaning that God tells us to go to a specific person or group of people at a specific time (as He did with Paul). Hold up your cell phone and state that it is like this cell phone. God is on one end, and we are on the other. Dial the number of the phone that the other person in your group has. When your students hear the phone ring, they'll be surprised. After the other person answers the phone, tell him or her to go outside and head to the drinking fountain (or whatever fits your setting).

Share that sometimes we do receive specific instructions from God, but often He works through a general calling, meaning God's call to all Christians at all times. Hold up the megaphone and state that a general calling is like this megaphone. God calls out to every person who has committed his or her life to Him. The Bible is full of these types of callings. Choose four volunteers to read the following Scriptures: Matthew 28:18-20; Matthew 5:13-16; Mark 1:16-18; John 17:18. Ask students to try to paraphrase what they have read in their own words. Now discuss the following questions:

- Of all these verses, which one is the most meaningful to you? Why?
- Would you rather have a general calling or a specific calling? Why?
- In your experience, how does God normally speak to you—through verses in the Bible to all believers or through a specific sense of what He wants you personally to do?

Explain that God speaks more often through His general calling. Therefore, we don't have to wait around to have a vision like Paul had. We can get moving right now.

Option 2: Tim the Firefighter. For this option, you will need the story found in this option and some Bibles. Read the following to your group members:

Tim loved firefighting. Well, at least he thought he would love firefighting. He had never actually done it, but he had practiced for it, been through firefighting school, and had all the equipment he needed.

He even lived at the firehouse with the other firefighters. Day after day, a voice would come over the loudspeaker and say, "Attention, all firefighters! We have a fire emergency. Report to your fire truck immediately!" At that point, all the firefighters would drop whatever they were doing and throw on their fireproof jackets, boots and helmets. Then they would slide down the pole and hop on their fire trucks. All but Tim, that is. He would never go with the rest of them.

Finally, the fire captain asked him what was going on. "Why don't you ever go when we're called?" he asked.

Tim explained, "My name is Tim, and the voice on the loudspeaker has never said my specific name. When it does, I'll go, but until then, I think I'll just wait."

Ask the students if they think Tim seems like a lame firefighter. What's wrong with him? He doesn't realize that the orders for "all firefighters" also apply to him. In the same way, when we hear stories from the Bible we sometimes think, *Sure, that's great for that person. He or she was some super-spiritual hero and knew exactly what God wanted him or her to do. But I haven't seen God in any visions lately or heard Him speak out loud to me. How do I know what I'm supposed to do?* In fact, God speaks to us in two ways: (1) a specific calling, meaning that God calls us to a specific person or group of people at a specific time; and (2) a general calling, meaning God's call to all Christians at all times.

Choose four volunteers to read the following verses: Matthew 28:18-20; Matthew 5:13-16; Mark 1:16-18; John 17:18. After each verse, ask the students to give a brief summary of what they think the passage is saying. Then ask the following questions:

- Which of these verses stuck out to you the most? Why?
- What is the difference between a general calling and a specific calling?
- Which would you rather receive? Why?
- How does God normally speak to you? Does He speak to you through His Word, through other Christians, through an impression of what He wants you to do, or in some other way?

Explain that God speaks more often through His general calling, so we don't have to wait around to have a vision or hear an audible voice. We can get moving right now!

APPLY

Option 1: My Friends. For this option, you will need copies of "My Friends" (found on the next page) and pencils. Explain that God's voice in Scripture has already called us to share the gospel with others. Ask the group how knowing this should change our lives.

Distribute pencils and copies of "My Friends." Explain that the students will need to make a list on the handout of all the people they sit near at school, the people they hang out with at lunch, and the people they are with after school. Give them a few minutes to make their lists, and then ask them to circle two of the names they have written down that they would like to share their faith with for the next month.

Following this, have them write down two things they can do to obey God's call to share the gospel with these people. Close by asking the group to consider how wonderful they think it would be if these two friends heard the gospel and maybe even accepted Jesus into their lives because the students heard God's voice and obeyed.

Option 2: Colorful Reminders. For this option, you will need some M&Ms or other colored candies, extra bags of M&Ms, paper and pencils.

Divide the students into as many groups as there are colors of candies and assign each group a color. As you distribute paper and pencils, explain that you are going to draw one candy at a time out of the bag that you are holding.

My Friends

Write down the names of all the friends and people you can think of who . . .

Sit near you at school

_____
_____
_____
_____

You hang out with at lunch

_____
_____
_____
_____

You spend time with after school

_____
_____
_____
_____

Circle the names of two people you would like to tell about Jesus in the next month. Write down two things you can do to share the gospel with them.

_____
_____
_____
_____

friend:

(1) a: one attached to another by affection or esteem; b: acquaintance (2) a: one that is not hostile; b: one that is of the same nation, party, or group; (3): one that favors or promotes something; (4): a favored companion.

When you pull one out, the team that has that color will need to write down the name of one person in their lives who doesn't know Jesus. It can be a friend, cousin, neighbor or teacher. After you have chosen a piece of candy, throw it to the group that has the same color.

Do this until each group has written at least three names down. After this, explain that you now want them to write down five ways they could be involved in helping these people meet Jesus. They can write down specific things they need to be praying for, what they could say to these people, or actions that would show these people about the love of Jesus.

Close in prayer, and then distribute a bag of candy to each student as a reminder of how they should be involved in helping others hear God's voice.

REFLECT

The following short devotions are for the students to reflect on and answer during the week. You can make a copy of these pages and distribute to your class or download and print from **www.gospellight.com/uncommon/jh_listening_to_God.zip.**

1—SEARCH AND RESCUE

Lost your way? Then check out Luke 19:10.

One of the places in America that hikers get lost the most is in the Sipsey Wilderness in northwest Alabama. Each year, search and rescue teams perform anywhere from 85 to 100 missions. Many of these people get lost because they don't follow directions or because they don't prepare well enough before they start out. In spite of this, the rescue teams *always* go out when someone is lost.

Jesus is the ultimate search-and-rescuer for all of humankind. Look up what He says about Himself in Luke 19:10 and fill in the blanks:

For the ____ ___ _____ [Jesus] came to _____ and to _____ what was
_____.

Jesus left heaven and came here to earth to seek and save the lost. Who do you think are "the lost"?

_____

_____

_____

According to Romans 3:23, *all* have sinned, so *everyone* is lost. That means every person, including *you*. Jesus came to find you and save *you*. But He also came to find and save your friends and relatives. But how will they know about what He has done for them—the good news? That's where you come in. You get to tell them. God doesn't have any other plan to get the good news out to others. He uses people just like you to bring others to Christ.

2—LOST SHEEP

One day, Jesus told a story about a lost sheep. Read about it in Luke 15:1-7. What did the shepherd do when he lost that one single sheep?

- ❏   Said, "Whew! Glad I've got 99 more!"
- ❏   Searched for the sheep until he found it.
- ❏   Searched for the sheep for an hour or so, then went back home.
- ❏   Called his younger brother to go look for it.

Who is the Shepherd in the story? Who are the lost sheep?

_____

_____

_____

God cares about those who are lost and goes out in search of them. And He calls you to go in search of them as well. Today, think about who the "lost sheep" are in your life and how you can bring them to Jesus.

3—SHEEP, WOLVES, SNAKES AND DOVES

Jesus referred to people as sheep on more than one occasion. Look up Matthew 10:14-16. In this passage, Jesus was sending out His 12 disciples to heal the sick and share the good news with the people in the area. He wanted to give them some instructions before they left. What does He say the disciples are like?

- ❏   Sheep among wolves
- ❏   Doves among snakes
- ❏   Wolves among sheep
- ❏   Sheep among snakes

What does He tell them to do?

- ☐ Be as strong as wolves and innocent as doves
- ☐ Be as innocent as doves and meek as sheep
- ☐ Be as shrewd as snakes and innocent as doves
- ☐ Be as sheepish as doves and snaky as wolves

Jesus knew that not everyone would be open to what they were saying—that what He was asking them to do wouldn't always be easy. But He sent them out just the same, just as He sends you out. If you told one person about Jesus, but he or she didn't want to listen, what would you do next?

_____

_____

_____

Spend a few minutes in prayer, and ask God to help you to pray for this person. Ask Him to soften that person's heart and to create the right time and place for you to tell him or her about Jesus.

4—HARVEST TIME

Each of us has been called to share the good news of Christ, but sometimes God gives us different tasks to do. Read John 4:35-37. What are "the fields"? How are they "ripe for harvest"?

_____

_____

_____

What does the sower do? What does the reaper do?

_____

_____

_____

Sometimes, God will call you to plant "seeds" of the gospel into your friend's life. However, remember it *isn't your job to save the person.* Just like you can't make a seed grow into a plant, so too you can't make a person accept Christ. That is the Holy Spirit's job, and you can count on Him to do His part! You just need to be ready and willing to share God's love when He calls you to do so.

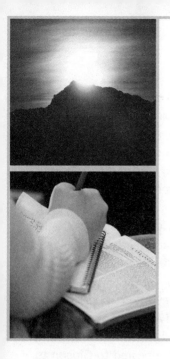

HOW DOES GOD SPEAK IN THE BIBLE?

In this first unit, we've examined several ways that God speaks to us today. We've discussed how God communicates through His Word (the Bible), how He guides us in our daily lives, how He gives us vision and strength, and how He transforms our lives and empowers us to share the gospel with others. But what about back in biblical times? How did God let people know what He wanted them to do? What methods did He use to communicate? Let's look at a few key examples from Scripture.

The first method that God used was an *audible voice*—people actually heard Him speak to them. One of the best examples is found in 1 Samuel 3, where God calls to Samuel, a young boy living in the Temple with the priest Eli. When Samuel hears the voice, he thinks it is Eli and runs off to ask what the old man wants. Twice the priest tells Samuel that he didn't call and sends him back, but on the third occasion he clues in and tells Samuel to say, "Speak, LORD, for your servant is listening" (verse 9). When Samuel does, God relays a message to him. In the New Testament, God spoke audibly to Paul on the road to Damascus (see Acts 9:4-5).

God often spoke to people through the *counsel* of men and women of God. We find this numerous times in the Old Testament when God sent prophets to warn people of what would happen if they didn't turn back to Him. At times, the prophets also spoke words of encouragement to individuals, as in 2 Samuel 7, where the prophet Nathan told King David what God had revealed to him after David stated his desire to build a Temple for the Lord. In the New Testament, a man named Agabus told Paul what the Holy Spirit had told him would happen to Paul when he went to Jerusalem (see Acts 21:11).

God not only used *dreams and visions* to deliver messages to His prophets (Ezekiel, Isaiah, Obadiah and John, the author of Revelation, among others) but also used these methods to speak to people who did not necessarily follow Him. In Genesis 41, Pharaoh, the king of Egypt, received two dreams that Joseph then interpreted; in Daniel 4, King Nebuchadnezzar had a dream that Daniel had to interpret. In the New Testament, God sent a dream to Joseph to tell him to take Mary as his wife (see Matthew 1:20-21), and Peter received a vision that instructed him to associate with non-Jews (see Acts 10).

In the Bible, *angels* are God's messengers, and they often appear on the scene to communicate a word from God. Angels visited Abraham and told him that he and Sarah would have a son (see Genesis 18), Lot received a warning from angels to flee Sodom (see Genesis 19), an angel appeared to Gideon to encourage him with a message from God (see Judges 6), and an angel visited Daniel after some delay to tell him what God had said in answer to his prayer (see Daniel 10). In the New Testament, the angel Gabriel visited Mary and told her that she would give birth to Jesus (see Luke 1:26-38), an angel announced the resurrection of Jesus from the dead (see Matthew 28:5-7; Mark 16:6-7); Paul received a message from an angel while at sea (see Acts 27), and an angel revealed the words of Revelation in a vision to John (see Revelation 1:1; 22:8).

Finally, God revealed His word through *written Scripture*. When Joshua assumed leadership of the Israelites after Moses' death, he urged the people to "not let this Book of the Law depart from your mouth" (Joshua 1:8). The psalmist stated, "Your word is a lamp to my feet and a light for my path" (Psalm 119:105). And Paul told Timothy, "All Scripture is God-breathed and is useful for teaching, rebuking, correcting and training in righteousness" (2 Timothy 3:16).

Today, God wants to speak to us, and He will do so in many ways if we learn how to listen for His voice.

UNIT II

Obeying God's Voice

When I once asked a student in Sunday School what she was up to for the rest of the week, I was stunned by her answer.

"Well, not much, except for I'm going to the Buddhist temple on Tuesday night."

"Really?" I said. "Do you go there often?"

"Pretty much every week. I find that it really helps me, just like coming to Sunday School here."

Mind you that she was not some first-time guest. She was a student who had for years been coming to Sunday School, retreats, scavenger hunts, beach days and camps. In typical junior-high fashion, she had raised her hand several times at several different events to become a Christian. In fact, she believed she had accepted the Christian faith. Along with elements of the Buddhist faith, that is.

If you spend much time with junior-highers, you will quickly realize that their concept of faith—hearing God's voice and obeying what it says—is different than their parents (and probably even yours). Faith is something that makes them feel better in the here and now. Some days that might be faith in Jesus Christ, while other days it might be faith in Buddha, or their computer games, or their friends, or themselves. What feels right Monday at lunch can be completely different than Wednesday afternoon in their friend's room and Saturday morning watching TV.

That's why these sessions are so important—not because we're trying to paint a picture of following God's voice in a way that matches previous generations, but because we're trying to paint a picture that matches the truth that is spelled out rather clearly in God's Word.

Please spend time during these sessions to reinforce the differences between obeying God's voice as found in His Word and obeying the tenets of other religions. Clarify with your group members that it is impossible to believe that Christianity and other religions are simultaneously true. Christianity's emphasis on our human sin, the grace offered through Christ, and our need to respond separate it from all other efforts to reach (and in some cases, become!) God. While other religions encourage followers to seek after God, Christianity is one of the only faith systems that believes God seeks after us—that He speaks to us and calls us to follow Him.

According to Dr. J. P. Moreland, today's Church has confused the need for a childlike faith with childlike thinking. As a result, we have "lost, or neglected, the ability to *disciple the mind* for Christ," making faith and a disciplined mental life "natural enemies."[1] During this series, make sure you get past your students' half-hearted and half-minded Sunday School answers about their beliefs. Force them to dig deeper about how God speaks to them and what He has called them to do. Affirm them for their curiosity and questions about God, and give them the tools to find out the answers themselves in His Word.

Also, as you teach this study, do not cheat your students out of the time required to truly respond in the closing Apply step in each session. Give the Holy Spirit time to do the surgery He wants to do, removing students' false ideas about faith, following God and its impact on their lives. Allow Him to implant in them a new desire to have a faith that shakes them and the world around them.

Kara Powell
Executive Director of the Fuller Youth Institute
Assistant Professor of Youth, Family and Culture
Fuller Theological Seminary

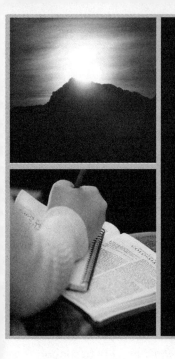

OBEYING GOD'S VOICE FOR SALVATION

THE BIG IDEA

Even in the midst of our sin, God rescues us when we obey His call to confess our sins and follow Him.

SESSION AIMS

In this session, you will guide students to (1) understand God's gift of salvation; (2) feel privileged to obey God's voice and accept this gift through faith; and (3) be faithful to Christ because of their relationship with Him.

THE BIGGEST VERSE

"For it is by grace you have been saved, through faith—and this is not from yourselves, it is the gift of God—not by works, so that no one can boast" (Ephesians 2:8-9).

OTHER IMPORTANT VERSES

Exodus 20; Matthew 5:14-16,21-30, 44; 6:2-4,6,9-21,25; 7:1-2; Romans 3:23; 5:8; 6:23; 10:8-10; 2 Corinthians 5:21; Ephesians 2:1-10; Colossians 1:13-14; Hebrews 11:25

Note: Additional options and worksheets in 8^1/$_2$" x 11" format for this session are available for download at **www.gospellight.com/uncommon/jh_listening_to_God.zip**.

STARTER

Option 1: Lean Two. For this option, you will need masking tape. Ahead of time, use two long pieces of tape to create the two sides of a triangle (leave the bottom open) on the floor in your meeting room.

Greet the students and divide them into two equal groups. Have each group make a line. The first person in each line should stand where the tape-lines touch. Have them face one another and tell them to put the palms of their hands out against each other. Next, have them see how far down the lines they can move keeping their hands together and without stepping off the tape. Allow each pair to try moving down the line. The winner is the pair that moves the greatest distance down the lines.

Ask the group what they thought was the key to being able to move all the way down the lines. (The answer should be that the pairs who leaned against each other for support were the ones that made it farther.) In order to do this, each person had to have faith that his or her partner would be able to support him or her to the end of the lines.

Explain that in the previous six sessions, we have been focusing on hearing God's voice. For the next six sessions, we will be focusing on how we can act on God's voice—how we can follow Him and believe that we have heard His calling on our lives. To do this requires *faith,* which means not only believing in God but also seeking His voice and leaning on Him for support.

Option 2: Stair Antics. For this option, you will need a building with a staircase (indoors or outdoors).

Greet the students and divide them into two teams. Have both teams line up at the bottom of the staircase. Have the teams stand in straight lines, with the first person in each team facing the staircase. The goal is for each team to get their entire team upstairs and downstairs again. Here are the rules:

- The first person must climb to the top of the staircase.
- Each person on the team must wait to ascend until the team member before him or her reaches the top step.
- The team must stay at the top of the stairs and cannot begin to descend until the last team member arrives at the top step.
- Each person on the team must wait to descend the stairs until the team member before him or her reaches the bottom step.
- Both teams must listen and follow any instructions given by you as they go.

Whether to have both teams compete at the same time will depend on how wide your stairwell is. If you do not have enough room for both teams, you can choose to have the teams go individually and compete for the best time. If you choose this option, make sure you give the same instructions to each team as they are playing to make the contest fair.

Begin the race. As the teams are ascending the stairs, call out silly instructions such as "go backward," "turn around every third step," or "go up on your hands and knees." Afterward, ask the students the following questions:

- Has anyone ever seen a duel on TV or in a movie? (*Of course!*)
- Did the men or women who were going to have the duel check their guns before they began? (*Usually!*)
- Why would they do that? (*Because they knew they had to trust their lives to their weapons and wanted to make sure they would work.*)
- Why didn't anyone think to check the stairs before our competition began? (*Huh?*)

Explain that the game they just played was about something we call "faith." During the previous six sessions, we discussed how we can hear God's voice. For the next six sessions, we will be focusing on how we can act on God's voice—how we can follow Him and believe that we have heard His calling on our lives. To do this requires faith, which means not only believing in God but also obeying what He is telling us to do. In the game, the group members had so much faith in the stairs that they put their full body weight on them without even thinking about it. They even did some goofy stunts on them! They believed the stairs would hold them up. In the same way, if we believe in God and what He is saying to us, we will act in ways that show we completely trust in Him.

MESSAGE

Option 1: Walking Zombies. For this option, you will need a package of index cards, kite string, scissors and a pen for each group of four to six students. You will also need several Bibles.

Divide the students into groups of four to six and distribute a set of supplies to each group. Have each person take at least one index card and a pen. Ask the group members to discuss the most common sins that junior-highers commit. (Some examples might be lying, fighting with parents, cheating on a test.) Have each student write a different sin than the rest of his or her group on one of the cards. Allow a few moments for the students to discuss and write, and then instruct them to turn the cards over and write a word that describes God. (Some examples might be "love," "grace," "peace.")

When everyone is finished, ask the teams to poke holes in the cards, making sure it is a large enough hole for the kite string to fit through. Have each student tie a card around his or her neck.

Ask students to raise their hands if they have ever seen a zombie movie. Choose a few volunteers to model how the zombies walked in the movie. Next, have the group members flip their necklace cards to the "sin" side. Tell them that while their sins are showing, they must walk like zombies. While they are walking around, you are going to read some Scripture verses, and if they hear the words "but because of His great love for us, God" while you are reading, they must freeze right where they are.

Read Ephesians 2:1-6 and watch for students to freeze when you read verse 4. After you have finished reading, explain that when we have faith in God, He brings us back to spiritual life. Ask the students to turn their cards around and to walk like someone who has just been brought back to life. As the students walk, read Ephesians 2:7-10. Next, discuss the following questions with the group:

- If you had to choose between being on earth as a zombie or as a real, living person, which would you choose and why? (*Hopefully a real, living person.*)
- What's the difference between being dead in sin and being alive in Christ? (*Being dead in sin means that our sin separates us from God and from experiencing His salvation. Being alive in Christ means that we have a relationship with Christ. Christ removes the sin that separates us from God so that we can be near to God, hear and obey His voice, and experience His salvation and plan for our life.*)
- What does Paul say in verse 3 that we deserve because of sin? (*We deserve God's wrath*).
- What does the word "wrath" mean? (*It means punishment for an offense or crime.*)
- What do verses 4, 5 and 7 say that God did for us? (*God, out of His great love, mercy, grace and kindness, made us alive with Christ even though we didn't deserve it.*)
- What does verse 8 say that faith has to do with it? (*Faith is the means through which we receive God's grace, obey what He is calling us to do,*

and are made alive. God didn't create us to walk like zombies; He intended
us to walk in new life. God gave us a tremendous gift in Jesus' death and
resurrection. All we need to do is have faith in order to receive the gift!)[1]

Conclude by stating that no matter how hard we try, we can't rescue ourselves from spiritual death. Obeying God's call to repent of our sins and believe in Jesus is the only way out! God gave us an amazing gift—life forever with Him—and it is our faith in Christ that allows us to accept this gift.

Option 2: Set Me Free. For this option, you will need several Bibles, several rolls of masking tape, felt-tip markers, one large jar with a large opening, two small jars with small openings, water, a funnel and a few adult leaders to assist you during the meeting. Ahead of time, fill the large jar with water.

Explain that because of God's love and grace, He has given us His Word, which tells us what He has said we must do to receive eternal life. To receive this gift, we must obey His voice and accept Christ into our lives. Ask the group what the difference is between life with God and life without God. (The answer would be that even though we sometimes don't recognize it, huge differences exist between life with God and life without God—and faith is one of the keys.)

Next, distribute Bibles and choose a volunteer to read Ephesians 2:1-3. Explain that this passage is about the way we *used* to live and how the sin in our lives made us spiritually dead. Because of this sin, we were separated from God. We would not allow God to speak to us or work in us or through us.

Ask the students to put their hands together as if they were going to clap. Give each adult leader a roll of masking tape and a felt-tip marker. Send the leaders out to tape each student's hands together and to write the word "SIN" on the tape with a marker. When everyone has his or her hands taped, ask the students to do a series of simple activities, such as giving others high fives or straightening up the room. Allow a minute or two for them to try doing what you ask. Then ask the group if they thought it was difficult to do these tasks.

Youth Leader Tip
If you have adult leaders, ask them to help you do things like tape kids' hands together or pass out supplies. It gets them involved, helps students see them as servants, and frees you up to continue teaching.

Explain that just as the tape kept them from doing what you asked, sin keeps us from doing what God asks. If they tried to pull the tape off and do what you asked, they probably would succeed. Undoing our sin is another story. Without faith in Jesus Christ, our spiritual bondage is so tight that not only is it impossible to free ourselves, but also we wouldn't even think to try.

Choose a volunteer to read Ephesians 2:8-9. Hold up the two smaller jars and explain how we are like these small jars—we are empty. Next, hold up the large jar. State that the larger jar represents God. God is filled with love, grace, mercy, kindness, life, and more. Often, we don't even know we're missing those things, but God, in His infinite love and wisdom, wants to fill us up with life, free us from sin and use us to do good. Hold one of the small jars up against the large one. State that the problem is that our God won't force Himself into our lives. Hold up the funnel. Explain that He provided a means to pour His love, grace and mercy into our lives—a way in which we can accept His gift of salvation. That way is through faith in His Son, Jesus Christ. When we follow God's voice and accept His plan of salvation, He frees us from our sins.

Insert the funnel into the opening of one of the small jars and choose one student volunteer. Remove the tape from the volunteer's hands and ask him or her to use the funnel to pour some of the water from the large jar into the smaller one. Then have the volunteer fill up the other small jar as well. Point out that though both small jars are full, the large one still isn't empty because God always has enough to fill us up!

Explain that when we have faith in Jesus and believe that He died on the cross and came back to life, God, by His grace, rescues us from sin and makes us alive in Christ. Our faith is the funnel through which God pours Himself into our lives. Have the adult leaders remove the tape from the students' hands. Conclude by explaining that in Ephesians 2:7-10, Paul tells us that God, because of His love, gave us a tremendous gift. In the same way that God physically raised Jesus from the dead, God has raised us from spiritual death to new life with Christ. All we have to do is obey His voice and accept this gift.

DIG

Option 1: How Good Is Your Gum? For this option, you need one piece of individually wrapped sugar-free bubble gum for each student and a timing device.

Distribute one piece of gum to each person and have each group member find a partner. Explain that in the following game, they are going to brag to their partners about how incredibly wonderful they are because of their delicious bubble gum. The partner with the longest thumb can go first. Allow the first set of partners to brag for 15 seconds, and then have the other set of partners brag for 15 seconds. Afterward, discuss the following questions:

- How did it feel to brag about yourself? (*Some students probably felt awkward, while others probably thoroughly enjoyed it!*)
- What did you do to earn the piece of gum? (*Nothing.*)
- Did it seem honest or dishonest to take credit for what I had given you? (*Allow students to answer.*)
- What have you done to deserve God's gift of salvation? (*Nothing! See Ephesians 2:8-9.*)
- How was taking credit for the gum like taking credit for salvation? (*Neither one was earned.*)

Explain that God has spoken to us through His Word and told us what we must do to be saved and experience His gift of eternal life. This gift of salvation is much greater than your gift of gum. We can't take credit for God's gift, but through faith we can enjoy it.

Option 2: A Thank-you Note. For this option, you will need just this book. Share the following case study with your group:

Tina was surprised when she got home and found a card from her grandmother in the mail. Her grandmother lived three hours away, and Tina hadn't seen her in a while. In fact, Tina was so busy practicing with her team she hadn't even talked to her grandmother recently.

Tina was shocked when she opened the card and a $100 bill fell out. She was totally excited and sat down to write her grandmother a letter. "Dear Grandma," she wrote. "You must think I'm the best granddaughter in the world. Well, you're right! I deserve the money because I'm good at school and I'm a really good athlete. I listen to my parents most of the time (except when they ask me to clean my room—then I shove everything under my bed so it only looks clean).

"Grandma, I know I don't call you often or ever write, but you obviously still think I'm great because you sent me money. I think I'll use it to buy a new outfit for school. I'm pretty popular, but it always helps to keep up with the very latest trend.

"Your loving granddaughter, Tina."

Now discuss the following questions:

- How do you think Tina's grandmother will feel when she receives Tina's letter? (*Probably sorry she sent the money to such an ungrateful brat!*)
- Why do you think Tina's grandmother sent her the money in the first place? (*Because she loves Tina.*)
- Did Tina deserve the money? Did she do anything special to earn it? (*No, she did nothing to earn it.*)
- How is Tina's response to her grandmother's gift similar to the way some people respond to God? (*Some people think they can earn salvation from God. They thank God for recognizing how great they are instead of thanking God for an undeserved gift.*)
- What would be a better way to respond to God? (*To accept His gift with gratefulness.*)

Explain that rather than boasting, Tina should have written a simple but sincere thank-you note. She could still have purchased a new outfit and then called or written her grandmother to tell her about the cute new clothes that the gift of money enabled her to buy. Her grandmother would have wanted to know that Tina appreciated and enjoyed the money. In the same way, God wants us to appreciate and enjoy His salvation. He wants to know that we have listened to His voice and obeyed what He has told us to do. However, we must approach Him with humility, because there is nothing we have done or ever could do to *earn* this amazing gift.

APPLY

Option 1: Bridging the Gap. For this option, you will need several Bibles for the students to use in the meeting, several Bibles that you will give to students as gifts, copies of "Bridging the Gap" (found on the next page), two phone books (or other large, sturdy books) and a 2 x 4-foot board. Ahead of time, place the two phone books on the floor at the front of the room with a large amount of space between them. Put the board off to the side until you need it.

Ask the group members if any of them can remember a time when they were really sick and felt as if they were never going to feel well again. Explain that we act differently when we're sick than we do when we're well. We can't do the things we enjoy. We just lay around moaning and groaning and hating life. That's much like the difference between being dead in sin and alive in

THE GAP OF SIN

There is no one righteous, not even one; there is no one who understands, no one who seeks God. All have turned away, they have together become worthless; there is no one who does good, not even one (Romans 6:10-12).

SPIRITUALLY DEAD

For the wages of sin is death, but the gift of God is eternal life in Christ Jesus our Lord (Romans 6:23).

JESUS BRIDGED THE GAP

For Christ's love compels us, because we are convinced that one died for all, and therefore all died. And he died for all, that those who live should no longer live for themselves but for him who died for them and was raised again (2 Corinthians 5:14-15).

CROSS THE GAP

If you confess with your mouth, "Jesus is Lord," and believe in your heart that God raised him from the dead, you will be saved (Romans 10:9).

Christ. Being alive in Christ means that we can do things for Jesus that we couldn't do when we were dead in sin.

Distribute "Bridging the Gap" and choose a volunteer to read the first Bible passage under the heading "The Gap of Sin." Direct the group members' attention to the two phonebooks on the floor. Have the group imagine that the book on the left is God and that the book on the right is us. The space in between represents the gap or deep canyon (like the Grand Canyon) that exists between us and God. That gap is sin.

Choose a volunteer to read the second Bible passage under the heading "Spiritually Dead." Explain that Paul tells us in Ephesians 2:1-3 that because of our sin, we are already spiritually dead. However, God has spoken His words of life into our hearts and has given us the gift of salvation through our faith in Jesus.

Choose a volunteer to read the third Bible passage under the heading "Jesus Bridged the Gap." State that while we have sinned and only deserve death, God loved us so much that He allowed Jesus to die in our place. Lay the board across the top of the phone books to create a bridge. Explain that the board represents Jesus. His death and resurrection made a bridge over the gap of sin that was between God and us.

Choose a volunteer to read the fourth Bible passage under the heading "Cross the Gap." Explain that in order to accept God's gift of salvation, we must believe and act on what He has said to us—that is what faith is. We need to believe in our hearts that when God said He raised Jesus from the dead, He actually did; and we confess that Christ is Lord of our lives. Walk across the board. Explain that when we do this, we have access to eternal life with God.

Close by inviting anyone who has not accepted Jesus as his or her Lord and Savior to begin a relationship with Jesus right now. Pray a short prayer, inviting God to work in the students' hearts and to help them have faith in Him. When you are finished, ask students to remain quiet with their eyes closed. Have them think about what they have learned today. Be sure to invite anyone who just accepted Jesus into his or her life to come and see you after the session. Give each of them a gift Bible and make sure to get their names, phone numbers and email addresses so you can follow up with them sometime in the next three days or so.

Option 2: A Valuable Gift. For this option, you will need scissors, green paper and pens or pencils. Ahead of time, cut the paper into pieces approximately the size of a dollar bill.

Begin by having your students imagine what it would be like if you gave them $100 every time they came to youth group. Then discuss the following questions:

- If I were to do this, would you tell your friends about it? (*Absotively! That's absolutely and positively!*)
- How valuable is the gift of eternal life? (*So valuable that it can't be measured.*)
- So why do we sometimes shy away from telling others about Jesus and His priceless gift of eternal life in heaven? (*Because we don't know what to say, we're afraid people will make fun of us, or it's hard to bring it up.*)

Distribute the green paper and pens or pencils. Ask the group members to think about someone they know who needs to hear God's voice in their lives and respond to the good news about Jesus. Encourage them to write that person's name on the paper. Ask them to put the paper in a place where they will see it regularly this week (a bathroom mirror, inside a locker, next to their computer) as a reminder to talk with that person (and others) about the amazing gift of eternal life he or she can have through a relationship with Jesus Christ.

REFLECT

The following short devotions are for the students to reflect on and answer during the week. You can make a copy of these pages and distribute to your class or download and print from **www.gospellight.com/uncommon/jh_listening_to_God.zip**.

1—YOU CAN'T EARN A GIFT

Gimmie, gimmie! Looking for a present? You'll find one in Ephesians 4:7.

Wow. Susan had just had the weirdest birthday *ever*! For months she had been looking forward to her thirteenth birthday, and lately her mom and stepdad were acting as if they had a really big surprise for her on her special day.

The day finally arrived, and when Susan came downstairs, she found a brand-new computer waiting for her *and* the amazing stereo system she'd been wanting *and* a huge television for her bedroom! This was much more than Susan had ever expected.

When she started to take the bows off her presents, her mother stepped in front of her and said, "Whoa! Not so fast! These *are* your birthday presents, but you won't get them until you've earned them by doing chores."

What would you say to your parents if you were Susan?

_____

_____

_____

Do you think it is right for Susan's parents to make her earn her presents? Why or why not?

_____

_____

_____

There are many people who think they have to earn the gift of forgiveness and grace from God. They seem to forget that God gave it as a gift. It *can't* be earned. In your prayers today, thank God for His present of salvation that you don't need to earn. Also pray for others who need this gift as well.

2—PAYBACK

Imagine you owed your friend a lot of money. You know that you need to pay her back before things will ever be "normal" between you again. What would you do to earn the money to pay her back?

- ☐ Mow pools and clean lawns (wait, I think that's the other way around).
- ☐ Go down to the docks and juggle, juggle, juggle!
- ☐ Babysit the Thompson twins and the Teter triplets
- ☐ Wash Mrs. Liberian's cats—all of them: Mitsui, Tatiana, Ms. Princess Meow-Meow and Tuffy.

Some people believe they can earn a pass to heaven if they work hard enough and are very good. Look up Romans 3:23. What do we earn because of our sins?

_____

_____

_____

What gift does God give us freely?

_____

_____

_____

Take a few moments to think and pray about God's gift of salvation and what it means in your life.

3—YOU ARE WORTH IT

Jump feet first into 1 Thessalonians 5:9-11!

It was one of the last days of summer camp. Mikey was thinking about some pretty serious things. His friend Darius had invited him to spend two weeks at church camp with him in the mountains, and even though Mikey wasn't a Christian, he said yes. The time in the mountains with Darius and the rest of the kids had been more fun than Mikey had ever had. They went swimming in the lake, spent late nights talking in the cabin, and Mikey even won a hotdog-eating contest.

Every night there was a church meeting in the big log cabin at the center of camp. At first Mikey just sat through them and thought of other things. However, toward the end of camp, he started to think about what he heard at the meetings. *Does God really speak to me?* Mikey wondered. *I don't think I'm even worth God's time.*

What would you say to Mikey to convince him that God does care about him?

_____

_____

_____

What would you say to show him that God wants to speak to him?

_____

_____

_____

_____

None of us will ever, ever, *ever* be "good enough" to *earn* the gift God wants to give us. Never! That is what is so cool about getting a gift. We can't earn it—and we don't have to! It's free! All God wants in exchange is for us to believe in Him and to accept His grace and forgiveness! So take time today to thank God for His gift to you.

4—GRATITUDE

Run, don't walk, to 2 Thessalonians 2:16-17.

One day, Theresa went to the mailbox and discovered a package from her grandmother. Inside was a sweater. There was also a note that read, "A gift for no other reason than the fact that I love you." Theresa's grandmother was on a fixed income, and Theresa knew it was a big deal for her to give Theresa such a nice gift.

Next week, her grandmother is coming for supper on Friday night. What should Theresa do?

- ❏ Mention the sweater is the wrong color and ask if her grandmother would mind if she returned it.
- ❏ Run to her grandmother's car as soon as it arrives to hug her, thank her and welcome her into the house.
- ❏ Hide out in her room until dinner, barely say anything during the meal, and return to her bedroom as soon as dinner is finished.
- ❏ Say, "Thanks, but I don't really need another sweater," and give the present back to her grandmother.

You have been given the gift of salvation, the greatest gift you will ever have. So today, ask God to help you have a thankful heart and never forget what it meant for Jesus to die on the cross for your sins.

OBEYING GOD'S VOICE FOR POWER

THE BIG IDEA

God gives us power in our lives when we listen for His voice and follow what He says.

SESSION AIMS

In this session, you will guide students to (1) understand that God works through people who listen to His voice; (2) feel motivated to ask God for power in their lives; and (3) pray for more faith before they even walk out of your room.

THE BIGGEST VERSE

"Everything is possible for him who believes" (Mark 9:23).

OTHER IMPORTANT VERSES

Psalms 27:14; 34:8; 50:14-15; Matthew 7:7-8; 17:20; Mark 6:7,13; 9:14-29; 10:27; John 14:14; 16:8; 2 Timothy 3:16-17; Hebrews 11:1; 1 John 1:8-9

Note: Additional options and worksheets in 8$^1/_2$" x 11" format for this session are available for download at **www.gospellight.com/uncommon/jh_listening_to_God.zip**.

STARTER

Option 1: Balloon Grab. For this option, you will need colored balloons, several markers and a whistle.

Greet the group members and clear a space in the center of the room. Give each person a balloon and a marker. Instruct the group members to blow up their balloons, tie them and write their names in very large letters on them. Let them know that when you blow the whistle, everyone must toss his or her balloon into the center of the room. As the balloons are flying around, students must try to keep track of where their balloons go. During this time, there are only two rules:

- No one can pop a balloon.
- No one can touch his or her own balloon until you blow the whistle for the second time (see below).

When you blow the whistle the second time, they must try to grab their own balloons as fast as they can. The last person to find his or her balloon must sit out the next round, but his or her balloon stays in the game.

Blow the whistle to begin. Allow a few moments of chaos before blowing the whistle to stop. Continue playing until you have a winner or for as long as time permits. Then discuss the following questions:

- What made this game difficult? (*Trying to keep track of my balloon while everyone else's was flying around.*)
- How could you recognize your own balloon? (*My name was on it.*)
- What things do junior-highers tend to focus on in life? (*Friends, physical appearance, computer games, clothes, popularity, grades, sports, and so on.*)
- What do adults tend to focus on? (*House, money, job, family, car, physical appearance, TV, and so on.*)

Explain that in order to stay in the game, all the players had to keep their eyes on their own balloons. Having faith is the same way. It means that we must keep our eyes focused on Jesus and listen to His voice even when distractions make it difficult.

Option 2: Guess the Photo. For this option, you will need several junior-high school pictures of yourself (and any adult volunteers).

Greet the students and ask them to form groups according to their eye color. Make sure you end up with an even number of groups. If you can't do eye color, choose hair color as an option. Assign each group a partner-group.

Explain that you are going to give each group a photograph of a well-known person. Ham it up so that students expect to see the picture of a celebrity. Give each group a picture of yourself (or an adult volunteer) as a junior-higher. Use different pictures for each group. Don't let the groups see each other's pictures or tell each other who is in their picture. Give the groups a moment to examine their pictures, and then have them describe what the person in the picture looks like to their partner-groups. Each group should try to guess who is in the picture of its partner-group.

After the guessing, allow students to pass the photos around and have a good laugh at your expense. When the ribbing subsides, discuss the following:

- How do you know what your friends look like? (*They are familiar to you.*)
- What if they changed their hairstyle or clothes—how would you know it was them? (*They would still have the same personality. You would be able to recognize them by who they are on the inside.*)
- If Jesus entered our room dressed like a junior-higher, how would you recognize Him? (*Allow for responses.*)

Explain that we recognize our friends because we have spent time with them. We know their faces, how they walk, how they act and how they talk. It is the same with Jesus. If we spend time with Him by reading the Bible and praying, we will get to know Him and be able to hear His voice when He speaks to us. We need to keep our eyes focused on Him so that we can recognize Him no matter what.

MESSAGE

Option 1: Tricky Puzzle. For this option, you will need several Bibles and a not-too-challenging three-dimensional puzzle game that students have to figure out. (One option might be an interconnecting nail puzzle, where the metal nails are oversized and bent to interconnect. The trick is to disconnect them. The nail puzzle can be purchased at most novelty game stores.) Ahead of time, be sure you know how to work the puzzle you choose!

Hold up the puzzle and ask the group if anyone thinks he or she can solve it. Select a volunteer whose hand *didn't* go up and who appears not to know how to solve the puzzle. Ask the volunteer to come forward. Invite him or her to try to solve it, even though you don't know if he or she can. Instruct the volunteer not to look away from the puzzle until you give the signal to stop. (*Note*: As always, when calling on someone who isn't the obvious choice for an activity, be sure to choose a person who is comfortable in the group. You don't want to humiliate or estrange a shy or new student just to make a point.)

While the volunteer works the puzzle, sit among the group and pantomime directions for solving it. If the volunteer follows your instructions and doesn't look away from the puzzle, he or she won't see your pantomime. Allow about three minutes for the student to work the puzzle and then give the signal to stop. If the volunteer has failed to solve the puzzle, invite him or her to try again, and tell the volunteer that you believe he or she can do it this time. Let the student know that he or she can now look away from the puzzle and watch you while trying.

When the volunteer is finished, distribute the Bibles. Have each student read one verse of Mark 9:14-29 aloud, and then discuss the following questions:

- Who failed in this story? (*The disciples [verse 18].*)
- Why did Jesus say they failed? (*Because they didn't pray [verse 29].*)
- Why couldn't [volunteer's name] solve the puzzle the first time through? (*He or she was focused only on the puzzle.*)
- How is praying like finding out the directions? (*Even though we don't always know where we're going, God always does. When we pray and ask for directions, God will lead us to where we need to be.*)

Explain that God wants to give us the directions and the power we need; all we have to do is keep our eyes focused on Jesus and listen to His voice. The father in this story brought his son to Jesus because he wanted Christ to heal the boy and to save his life (see verses 17-18,22). The father had some faith to begin with, and then he focused on Jesus and asked for more faith.[1]

Youth Leader Tip
Remember that vulnerability on your part will help build trust and memories in your junior-highers—even when being vulnerable means showing just how much you've changed since *you* were in junior high!

Ask the group members to think about how the puzzle game relates to the Bible story. Explain that the person we focus on and listen to makes a difference. In the case of the dad, he focused on Jesus, and Christ healed the boy.

Option 2: Growing Faith. For this option, you will need several Bibles, one packet of seeds and a large rock.

Distribute the Bibles and choose volunteers to read Mark 9:14-19,28-29 aloud. State that Mark 6:7 and 13 says that Jesus had given the disciples His authority to cast out evil spirits, and that they had done so successfully in the past. However, on this occasion it was different. They were unable to cast out the evil spirit from the boy.

Ask the group what they would have done if they were Jesus' best friend and disciple and had failed. (Some answers would be that they would have prayed or found Jesus to help them.) Explain that instead, Mark 9:14 points out that the disciples argued with the teachers of the law, even after a crowd had surrounded them. In fact, they argued so much that if television reporters had been around back then, they might have made it on the 6 o'clock news!

Ask the group members what reason Jesus gave to the disciples for their failure. Point out that Mark 9:29 says they failed to pray. Explain that prayer is how we communicate to God, hear His voice and plug into His power! The disciples forgot that the power to cast out demons was *God's* power, not theirs. The disciples could have healed the boy if they had realized this and prayed.

Hold up one of the packets of seeds and pour out a few into your hand. Ask for a show of hands of those students in the group who have grown plants from seeds. Ask those who raised their hands the following questions:

- What did you do to make it grow? (*You planted it in good soil, gave it plenty of light and watered it regularly.*)
- So, by doing these things, did you made the seed grow? (*No.*)

Illustrate your answer by holding up the rock. State that you have just found a neat rock. Have students imagine what would happen if you found a spot in your yard with sunlight, dug a hole, dropped the rock in and watered it every day. Would a mountain grow from that rock? Of course, the answer would be no. Why? Because God is the one who makes something grow or not grow. We can do all the right actions to make something happen, but it still can fail.

Read Mark 9:23 again. Explain that Jesus knew He could do anything, including healing the boy. He also knew that God wanted the boy to be healed.

However, in this case, Jesus wanted the father of the boy to experience the power of faith. The father offered his son and the small amount of faith that he had to Jesus. When Jesus told the father that everything was possible for a person who believes, the father said, "I do believe; help me overcome my unbelief!" (verse 24). Basically, the father was admitting that he had done all he could, and that he knew it wasn't enough.

Ask the group members how they think Jesus' healing the boy affected the father's faith. Did it make the father more willing to be obedient and follow what Jesus was saying to him? Allow the students to respond. Explain that Jesus didn't wait for the father to grow his own faith; He accepted the faith the father had and added to it. This should give us hope. We don't have to have it all together to come to God. Faith means knowing we don't have it together, but that we rely on the God who does.

DIG

Option 1: God's Voice and My Life. For this option, you will need copies of "God's Voice and My Life" (found on the next page), and pens or pencils.

Distribute the handout and pens or pencils. Instruct the group members to fill in the timeline on the left side of the handout with significant events that have taken place in their lives. On the right side, they should write things they would like to see God accomplish through them in the future. (For example, they might write "my brother was born" on the left side, and "graduate from high school" on the right.) Point out that the accomplishments just need to be anything that God might want to do through them in their everyday lives.

Allow the group members to write for a few minutes and then ask them to graph the events in their lives that have had an impact on their relationship with God and hearing His voice. For example, they might have had an experience at a summer camp where they felt especially close to God and heard His voice, so they would indicate that as a high point on the graph. A low point might be if a student's parents got divorced, or any other trying time that impeded them from hearing God's voice.

Allow three minutes or so for students to work on their graphs. Next, discuss the following questions:

- What do you notice about your faith when you look at your graph?
- When have you felt like you had the most faith in your life?
- When was your faith weakest?

GOD'S VOICE AND MY LIFE

Timeline of Events

My past | My future

Today

My Relationship with God

Create a graph of your faith by writing down times or events when you felt especially close to God and heard His voice. Draw a line to represent the amount of faith you had during each event.

Total faith				
Lots of faith				
Some faith				
Little faith				
Event	_____	_____	_____	_____

- When you look at your graph, how do the events in your life seem to affect your ability to hear God's voice?
- What events have made it difficult to obey what you felt God was telling you to do?
- What kinds of things would you like to see God do in your life?
- How do you think those things will affect your faith?

Conclude by stating that we grow in our faith when we listen to God's voice and follow what He says. As we are obedient and witness what He does in our lives, it builds our confidence and our faith in Him. The first step in this process is to ask for more faith, and then keep on praying.

Option 2: When God Says No. For this option, you will need your group of students and this book. (*Note:* This story is a bit of a downer, so be sensitive to the feelings of your group members before using this option. Pray that God will give you the wisdom to know what to say to kids who have questions about hurtful events in their lives.) Share the following story with the group:

James's parents bought him a Springer Spaniel named Freckles when he was just two years old. Every day around 3 PM, Freckles would sit on the front doorstep and wait for James to get off the school bus. He would lie on James's feet and wait patiently for James to get his homework finished every evening. He would run next to him as James rode his bike down the street to the park where they played Frisbee. On weekends, they would hike together through the canyon near their home.

One day when James returned from school, Freckles wasn't on the front porch. Worried, James looked for Freckles and found him hiding under the bed. He could tell the dog was sick. James picked him up and went with his dad to take Freckles to the vet. Although the doctor gave Freckles some medicine, he couldn't give James and his dad much hope. He sadly told them that Freckles didn't have long to live.

James thought about how he had heard in church that God did miracles when people prayed. So he prayed—a lot. He prayed when he brushed his teeth in the morning. He prayed before eating. He prayed when he gave Freckles his medicine. He prayed before he went to bed at night. James asked God to heal his best friend, and even told God he would do just about anything if Freckles got better.

But Freckles died anyway.

Discuss the following questions with the group:

- Have you ever been in a situation like this? (*Allow students to answer.*)

- Do you think God didn't heal Freckles because James didn't have enough faith? (*Freckles' death didn't have anything to do with James's faith. James did have faith. In this world, suffering and death are realities that we all have to face at some time. James has to trust in God's plan, even though he can't understand why Freckles wasn't healed.*)

- Why didn't God answer James's prayer and heal Freckles? (*God did answer James's prayer, but not in the way James wanted. This type of situation is hard for us to understand, because we can't see the bigger picture that God sees. There was a reason, but we don't know what it was.*)

- How do you think James should respond to this situation? (*He should honestly tell God how he feels, whether those are good or bad feelings. God can take it. He should ask God for comfort as he goes through this extremely sad time.*)

- Do you think God can use even this sad event to give James more faith? (*Allow students to respond.*)

Explain that James did everything right. He had faith God could heal Freckles, prayed about it and asked for healing. We need to understand that God doesn't always do the things we ask. God has a reason if He does not respond in the way we would want, but usually we will not know what it is. Regardless, we have to trust in God and continue to listen to His voice in our lives.

Explain that maybe the miracle God did was in James's life rather than in Freckles'. Maybe James learned more about prayer and built his trust in God even when things didn't work out as he wanted. God will make James stronger in his faith and continue to work through him. If James stops talking to God now, he will miss the gifts that God wants to give Him and the things He wants to do through him.

APPLY

Option 1: Taste and See. For this option, you will need your Bible and some tasty fresh-baked cookies.

Give each student a small piece of a cookie—just enough to tease them with a taste. As they salivate for more, read Psalm 34:8. Explain that in the same way that the students have tasted the cookies and now know how good they are, they have also gotten a taste of what God can do in their lives. State that it makes you happy to speak with the group members and be able to share the cookies with them, but it makes God even happier to be able to speak to them and share what He has with them. They only need to ask God.

Allow a moment of silence for the students to reflect on their relationships with God. Close in prayer, thanking God for His gift of faith and for speaking into each person's life. Ask God to help the group members know they can always come to Him and ask for anything, including faith. As the students leave, stand at the door and offer cookies to those who want them.

Option 2: Planting Seeds. For this option, you will need pens and one large seed for each person in the group (such as a sunflower or nasturtium seed).

Explain that some of the group members' friends might be like the father in Mark 9. They may feel desperately sad and hopeless because of their circumstances. They may know they need a miracle (though they may not say it that way), and they may even know they don't have what it takes to make things better, but they probably don't know where to go for help. In these situations, the group members need to know that they are the ones who can truly help those friends by showing them the way to Jesus. They can be the ones that God uses to speak His words of life into those friends' lives.

Distribute the seeds and explain that our job each day is to plant the seeds of the gospel in the people around us. We do this by sharing how much we really need Jesus and how much they need Him as well. As we share, we must remember that when we plant a seed, we can't make it grow—that is God's job. However, when we obey what He is telling us to do, we allow Him to work through us and, in the process, we grow in our own faith.

Ask the group members to think of one friend with whom they would like to share Jesus this week. Close in prayer, asking God to give them the faith to talk with their friends about Jesus and to give their non-Christian friends the faith to accept Jesus.

Youth Leader Tip

One of the most important investments of our energy is discipling young people to carry out the Great Commission. Your students *can* make a powerful difference for God, and God wants to use them for His kingdom today.

REFLECT

The following short devotions are for the students to reflect on and answer during the week. You can make a copy of these pages and distribute to your class or download and print from **www.gospellight.com/uncommon/jh_listening_ to_God.zip.**

1—AVERAGE TO AMAZING!

Christina is an average kid. She gets good grades, has average looks and does okay in gym class. She is not the most popular girl in school, but she has a few close friends. She has never wowed anyone on Sundays with a lovely singing voice or cracked anyone up in the skits performed on Wednesday nights in the youth group. She is pretty average.

So, how was this "pretty average" kid able to organize the most successful car wash in the church's history? When asked, Christina just shrugged her shoulders, smiled, and said, "It was all God, not me. I just felt it was something He was calling me to do. I guess you could say He organized the car wash."

God can do some truly amazing things through you when you let Him. When you listen to God's voice and do what He says, He will use you. What do you feel God calling you to do today?

_____
_____
_____

What, if anything, is preventing you from doing it?

_____
_____
_____

Do you have faith that if you do what God is telling you to do, He will be faithful to see it through? Why or why not?

_____
_____
_____

How will God use you today? Don't know? Then take a minute to pray about it!

2—WHO CAN YOU CALL?

Need some help? Then read Psalm 50:14-15, quick!

You are walking home from school one day, trying to figure out who you can ask to help you finish your presentation for English class. You are thinking about asking your dad. When you get home, you see that your dad is home early from work. He's doing dishes in the kitchen. Do you . . .

- ❑ Mumble a quick hello and then go to your room for a couple of hours, thinking that you'll ask him after dinner . . . maybe.
- ❑ Wave at him and then head to the couch in the TV room, thinking you will figure your project out yourself later.
- ❑ Say hello and then wait for him to ask if you need anything . . . then, when he doesn't, go to your room and sulk.
- ❑ Say hello and tell him how your day went, then tell him about the project and ask for help.
- ❑ Glare at him as he walks into the room and then march off to sulk, figuring that there's no point in asking him because he'll just say no.

When you need help, do you ask God, or do you try to take care of things yourself?

_____

_____

_____

What does Psalm 50:14-15 say we should do when we are in need of help?

_____

_____

_____

God is always ready to help you. So if you need help, go to Him now and talk to Him.

3—STEP OUT

What is faith, anyway? Check out Hebrews 11:1.

Andrew just doesn't get this faith thing that everyone is talking about all the time. At church, they won't stop talking about how it's supposed to help him move mountains and break down walls. Andrew knows he is a Christian. In fact, he has been one since he was five. He accepted Jesus on the front steps of his house with his mom. But he had trouble seeing how having faith that God will do something will actually bring it to pass.

If you were Andrew's friend, what would you say to him?

_____

_____

_____

_____

Fill in the words of Hebrews 11:1 below:

_____ is being _____ of what we _____ ____ and _____ of what we ___ _____ ____.

If you go on to read the rest of Hebrews 11, you will find all kinds of examples about people in the Bible (like Noah, Abraham and Moses) who heard God's voice and did what He said, even though they didn't always know why. These people *stepped out in faith* and did what they felt God was calling them to do. The results? God accomplished amazing things through them.

He will do the same for you in your life. If you show a little faith and decide to step out and act on that faith, God will bless you and give you more faith. So today, ask God to help you understand faith a little bit better, and then don't be afraid to take that first step!

4—PRAY, WAIT, PRAY, WAIT

Nobody likes to wait. So get moving and read Psalm 27:14.

Imagine you are baking bread. The dough is ready and sitting there in the pan. However, it is flat, because you had to mash it down and knead it. To get it to rise again, what do you think you should do?

- ❑ Dance around the pan, singing, "Rise and be bread!"
- ❑ Take the pan for a walk through the park.
- ❑ Go swimming with the bread dough (don't forget your towel).
- ❑ Do nothing.

The answer is do nothing! It takes time for the bread to rise. You just have to wait. Why is waiting hard to do sometimes?

_____

_____

_____

_____

When you pray, do you wait patiently for God to answer, or do you give up if you don't get an answer right away? Why?

_____

_____

_____

_____

We live in what is known as a "convenience-driven" culture. That is, we want things now and don't like the hassle of having to wait. But God doesn't work that way. What is one area of your life where you feel God is acting slower than you would like?

_____

_____

_____

_____

Today, give that area of your life over to God and ask Him to speak to you and maybe show you why you are having to wait. Then thank Him that His timing is always perfect!

OBEYING GOD'S VOICE AND DOING GOOD

THE BIG IDEA
When we follow God and obey His voice, we will want to do good deeds.

SESSION AIMS
In this session, you will guide students to (1) understand the importance of following God and how it affects their lifestyle; (2) become motivated to do good deeds; and (3) treat others as Jesus would because of their faith in Him.

THE BIGGEST VERSE
"Faith by itself, if it is not accompanied by action, is dead" (James 2:17).

OTHER IMPORTANT VERSES
Psalm 5:12; Proverbs 16:2; Isaiah 64:6; Matthew 7:24-27; 21:28-31; John 3:16; 5:19-20; 14:7; 15:4-6; Romans 3:28; 5:8; 1 Corinthians 11:20-22; 2 Corinthians 9:7; Ephesians 2:8-9; Colossians 3:12; Hebrews 1:8-9; James 1:22-24; 2:14-19

Note: Additional options and worksheets in 8½" x 11" format for this session are available for download at **www.gospellight.com/uncommon/jh_listening_to_God.zip**.

STARTER

Option 1: Complete the Phrase. For this option, you will need a whiteboard, a whiteboard marker, index cards and pens or pencils. Ahead of time, write out the following two phrases on the whiteboard: (1) "Because I believe . . ." and (2) "I will . . ."

Greet the group members and distribute two index cards and a pen or pencil to each person. Point out the statements on the whiteboard. Instruct the group members to finish the first phrase by writing something they believe on one of the index cards. On the second index card, have them write down an action they can do physically. The two cards do not need to be related in any way, but they can be. An example would be: "Because I believe pizza is the best food ever" . . . "I will run screaming through my second period class."

Allow a few moments for the group members to fill out their cards. When they are finished, ask each person to find a partner. Have each student exchange his or her second (action) card with his or her partner. Then have each person in the pair read the first and second card that he or she now has. Have all the students change partners and repeat the process. They can switch partners three or four times.

Once you are finished, discuss the following questions:

- Why were some of these sentences so funny?
- Do you think the things people believe affect the way they live?

Explain that listening to God and following Him in faith means you believe in something and then do it. Today, the group will be learning that when you believe God has saved you from sin and death, it will change your life and your actions will be different.

Option 2: Raise It Up. For this option, you will need three adult volunteers, a 2-foot by 8-foot wooden board, three sturdy chairs and a blindfold. Ahead of time, lay the board across two of the chairs. Meet with the two adult volunteers and have them practice "raising" the board off the two chairs while supporting it. The idea is to move slowly from a standing position to a crouching one so that the person standing on the board will have the impression of being raised above the heads of the two who are holding the board.

Greet the group members and choose three daring volunteers. Ask an adult volunteer to escort two of the student volunteers out of the room. Have the third student stand in front of the board across from two of the chairs. Blindfold the student and help him or her to climb onto the extra chair and then onto the board. Ask the two remaining adult volunteers to stand on either end of the board. Have the student volunteer reach out to touch the heads of the adults for support. Explain to the student volunteer that while he or she is standing on the board, the adults are going to raise it above their heads. When you give the signal, the student volunteer must jump off.

Signal the adult volunteers to "lift" the board. When the student volunteer can no longer touch the adults' heads, ask him or her to jump. The illusion of being high in the air will cause the volunteer to be afraid to jump—and if he or she does, it will be with trepidation at being so high in the air. Repeat the process with the other two volunteers, and then discuss the following questions:

- What did you think was happening when you couldn't reach the heads of the people who were holding the board?
- How high did you think you were when I asked you to jump?
- How did that belief affect the way you jumped?

Explain that our beliefs always affect what we do. This is also true regarding our faith. Today, we are going to discuss how following God's voice affects how we live.

MESSAGE

Option 1: Belief and Action. For this option, you will need several Bibles, scissors, one copy of "Belief and Action" (found on the next page) and a few small prizes. Ahead of time, cut the handout into individual cards.

Ask each person to form a trio with two other students from different schools (use a larger ratio if your group is bigger than 18 students). Distribute one "Belief and Action" card to each group. Explain that each group is going to come up with a pantomime that shows what someone might do if he or she had the

Youth Leader Tip

Our calling as youth leaders is to open the eyes of our students to see the needs right outside their doors. In this session, you will help your group members see that faith and works are linked—that doing good naturally flows out of having faith in God.

BELIEF AND ACTION

You believe basketball is the best sport.	You believe friends should spend time together.
You believe God loves you.	You believe you should help others.
You believe the Bible is God's Word.	You believe prayer has power.

belief written on the card. Allow a few minutes for the groups to work on their pantomimes. When they are ready, invite each group to perform while the rest of the students try to guess what is happening. When a student has guessed correctly, ask the rest of the students what belief they think is being shown. Give prizes to everyone just for playing.

After the presentations, discuss the following questions:

- Was it easy or difficult to guess what people believed based on their actions?
- How would you have been able to demonstrate what your belief was without actions?

Distribute the Bibles and choose a volunteer to read James 2:14-19. Then continue the discussion by asking the following:

- According to this passage, what does faith have to do with actions? (*Our actions show what we believe in—they show our faith.*)
- Why does verse 17 say that faith without action is dead? (*It is easy to say what we believe. It is much harder to prove it by our actions. We need to be willing to back our faith by doing what we believe is true.*)
- What would people think about our faith in Jesus if we didn't do anything that showed we believed it? (*They probably wouldn't believe it. Our actions wouldn't give them any reason to think that we were following Christ's voice or give them any reason to consider a relationship with Him for themselves!*)[1]

Explain that faith isn't just about listening to God and believing in Him, but it's also about obeying God's voice and acting on faith. You can't demonstrate what you believe without doing something. In fact, if you don't act differently because you believe in Jesus, then what you demonstrate is that you don't have faith in Jesus at all.

Option 2: Where's the Bread? For this option, you will need several Bibles, peanut butter, jelly, a knife and a way to clean it up.

Distribute the Bibles and choose two volunteers to help you make a peanut butter and jelly sandwich. Use the knife to spread a thin layer of peanut butter on one volunteer's hand, and then spread jelly on the other volunteer's hand. Instruct them to put their peanut butter and jelly hands together. Now choose another volunteer to read James 2:14-19 while the first two volunteers continue to hold their hands together. After the passage has been read, allow the volunteers to clean up. Discuss the following questions:

- How is making a peanut butter and jelly sandwich similar to faith without deeds? (*You don't have a sandwich without bread, and you don't have faith without good deeds.*)
- Why does faith have to be active? (*Faith without any action is dead [see verse 17].*)
- How would you feel about a person who saw a starving child, felt sorry for the child, wished the child had food, but then walked away and did nothing to help (see verses 15-16)? (*Allow students to answer.*)
- How can a person's actions demonstrate his or her faith? (*A person acts according to what he or she believes. If that person has faith and is really obeying God's voice, he or she will act in a way that shows it [see verse 18].*)
- What are some actions that would demonstrate a person's faith in Jesus? (*Allow students to answer.*)

Explain that when we make a sandwich, we need *bread*. In the same way, when we say we believe in Christ and are doing what He is telling us to do, we need to have the actions that match it. God doesn't want us to believe in Him with only our minds, but with our lives as well. Our faith in God has to be active, and it must make a difference in the way we live.

DIG

Option 1: Practice Makes Perfect. For this option, you will need several student or adult volunteers who play musical instruments. (*Note:* You will need to choose volunteers who won't mind letting someone else play or try to play their

Youth Leader Tip
Don't just read information to your students and hope they get the takeaway. Share personal stories with them to explain why certain points in Scripture are important to know and how they have changed your life.

instruments during the activity.) Ahead of time, arrange for the musicians to practice a short worship song and to be ready to play it for the group.

Have the musicians play the worship song, and comment about how well they played. Ask if anyone in the group would like to try playing one of the instruments. Randomly assign the instruments to the students, making sure that each person ends up with something that he or she doesn't know how to play. Invite the volunteers to try playing a song together, and be prepared to hear some pretty awful "music." Then ask the following questions:

- What was the difference between the two groups of musicians that played for the group? (*The first knew how to play their instruments; the second just winged it.*)
- What does a musician need to believe about practice in order to become skilled at playing an instrument? (*That practice will make him or her better.*)
- Why does it matter what we believe? (*Because what we believe will determine how we will live our lives.*)
- Why does it matter what we do? (*Because our actions can either make a difference in the world or can mess up our lives.*)

State to the group that what we believe (the Word of God) and what we do (the actions that come out of that belief) matters. It also matters that we share this good news with others.

Option 2: What's the Difference? For this option, you will need this book and a vision for what God wants to do in and through your students. Share the following story:

Jenny said she believed in God and she told her youth pastor that she was a Christian. However, her youth pastor was confused by the way Jenny acted. She was totally mean to other junior-highers at church. Sometimes she even swore at them if they made her angry.

Jenny wasn't having problems only at church. Her stepmother had called the youth pastor to talk about Jenny's behavior at school. Jenny had been caught stealing money from the student store last week. This week she had tried to cheat on her history test. In both cases, Jenny seemed to be more sorry that she had been caught rather than for what she had done.

Feeling completely helpless, Jenny's stepmom asked the youth pastor, "If Jenny were truly a Christian, wouldn't she be acting differently?"

Ask the students if they think Jenny was truly a Christian. Is it true that our actions show others what we really believe?

Explain that this is a tough question to answer. While it is true that our actions definitely reflect what we really believe, at the same time, no one is perfect. Even a Christian makes mistakes and sins. We need to hear Jesus' voice each day to help us live right and avoid temptation. Jenny might believe she's a Christian, but if she's not acting like she belongs to Jesus, it will be hard for others to see it. When we seek to follow God's voice and enter into a real relationship with Him, we will find that our actions will be different because our mindset will be different.

APPLY

Option 1: Good Fruit. For this option, you will need several Bibles, a banana for each student and pens.

Distribute the Bibles, bananas and pens. Choose a volunteer to read John 15:4-6. Explain that if a grapevine is healthy and it is getting enough nourishment from the soil and water and sunlight, it will produce good fruit. An unhealthy vine might still try to produce fruit, but it won't taste good. In the Bible, Jesus talks about vines to teach us something about ourselves. He wants us to know that if we have faith and are obeying what God is telling us to do, we will produce good deeds. Without faith, our deeds will be no good. We need to stay connected to Jesus in the same way that a branch must stay connected to the vine to remain healthy.

Ask the group members to think about the following questions:

- What kind of spiritual fruit have you been producing?
- What kind of spiritual fruit would you like to produce?
- What good deeds do you think God may be asking you to do?

Have the group members write their ideas on their bananas, focusing specifically on how they treat others. After everyone has written their ideas, invite them to peel their bananas and enjoy the good fruit inside. Close in prayer, asking God to continue to speak to the students and to help them do the good deeds He has asked them to do.

Option 2: Physical and Spiritual Help. For this option, you will need your Bible, index cards and pens or pencils.

Read James 2:15-16 to the group. Explain that one great way to share God's love with others is to give assistance to people who need help. When we do this, we will find that people will want to know what is different about us. This will give us the opportunity to tell them about Jesus Christ.

Distribute the index cards and pens or pencils. Divide the students into groups of four people each. Send one pair from each group to the left side of the room. Everyone on the left side will try to think of any *physical* needs junior-highers might have, such as a need for clothing. Send the other pair to the right side of the room. Everyone on that side will try to think of any *spiritual* needs junior-highers might have, such as a need to have God's peace. Each side can write their ideas on their index cards.

Allow time for the groups to come up with a list of ideas, and then have the pairs regroup and share their lists with their groups. Ask the groups to pick their favorite way to care for a physical need and to care for a spiritual need, and then write down these two ideas.

After everyone has had time to write his or her ideas, choose one person from each group to read the ideas aloud. When all groups have read, have the students pray silently. During this time, they should ask God to help them think of someone who needs physical or spiritual help in their lives. Close in prayer, asking God to give the group members a chance to help someone this week either physically or spiritually.

REFLECT

The following short devotions are for the students to reflect on and answer during the week. You can make a copy of these pages and distribute to your class or download and print from **www.gospellight.com/uncommon/jh_listening_to_God.zip.**

1—JUST A LITTLE KINDNESS

What's in your wardrobe? Do you need some new clothes? Take a look at Colossians 3:12.

Angie became a Christian at the beginning of the summer, but she sure hasn't changed much. She still spends her entire (very generous) allowance at the mall every Saturday. She still makes fun of anyone who isn't as cool as she is. She's still a brat to her parents and her little brother. For Angie, "being a Christian" is like being a part of a fun little club, but not much else.

What does Paul say in Colossians 3:12 about how we should act because we are "God's chosen people"?

_____

_____

_____

How loving are you to others? How do you show kindness to them?

_____

_____

_____

_____

It's not an easy thing, but God wants to give you the strength to love the people in your life. When you do that, they can see the love of God as well. Today, think of a person to whom you can really show love. Maybe it's your mom or a new kid at school. Figure out a way to do something really great for that person, and go do it!

2—WHAT CAN I DO?

Oh no! Your friend just called to tell you that your pastor's house has burned down! What are you going to do?! Circle one of the responses below:

- ❑ Huh? What am *I* going do? It's the pastor's problem, not mine. I'm just a kid; the pastor and his wife are adults. They can take care of themselves.
- ❑ What juicy gossip! I'm going to call everybody I know and tell them what happened!
- ❑ Oh no! That's horrible! Sure wish I could do something. I'm pretty busy right now, though.
- ❑ Wow, I'd better start praying for them. When my dad comes home from work, I'll ask him what we should do to help.

How do you tend to react when a Christian friend needs help? Do you get busy with other things or do you jump in and try to help?

_____

_____

_____

Is there someone in your life who could use some help? Maybe there's a single mom who could use some babysitting or just a friend who needs someone to talk to. Take the time to help someone today.

3—GIVE TILL IT FEELS GOOD

So, we know we should be giving to others and helping them out. But does it matter if we are happy about it? Second Corinthians 9:7 should shed some light on the subject.

It was a day for giving. Tina could feel it in her bones as soon as she woke up. She let her little brother have the last English muffin. She did the dishes for her mother without being asked. At school, she let Angie borrow her math book and gave Peter the apple from her lunch. After school, Tina saw a homeless woman digging through the trash can outside a fast-food place. She bought the woman a sandwich and a bag of chips. Yep, it was a giving day all right.

Would you describe Tina as a cheerful giver?

_____

_____

_____

Now read Matthew 21:28-31. This passage of the Bible is known as the Parable of the Two Sons. What was the difference between the two sons?

_____

_____

_____

God wants a cheerful giver, but He also wants people who will *follow through on what He asks them to do.* In everything we do, we need to remember that part of the reason God is generous to us is so that we can be generous to others. We can show kindness because He has shown kindness to us.

4—A TOUGH QUESTION

It's time for youth group, which you love. The games are silly and fun, the volunteers are really cool and the teaching time isn't boring (usually). And, of course, there are kids to hang out with. You see four people as soon as you walk in the door. Who do you say hi to first?

- ❏ Thomas, a skater with a shaved head, huge pants and a backpack over his left shoulder
- ❏ Liz, a quiet girl you don't really know
- ❏ Stanley, a kid whose parents are missionaries and who just got back from China
- ❏ Chris, the most popular kid in the whole group

Read 1 Corinthians 11:20-22. As you can see, Paul had some strong words for the way that people were acting in this church. What were the two groups in this church?

_____

_____

_____

_____

What was the first group doing that didn't show much kindness to the other group?

_____

_____

_____

_____

Do you treat everyone the same, or do you pay more attention to certain people? How do you treat other Christians? How do you think you should treat them? What would you need to change in your life to treat others in a better way this week? Today, think about these questions and ask God to show you any way you are not treating others with the kindness that God has shown to you.

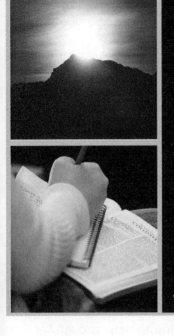

OBEYING GOD'S VOICE IN TIMES OF WAITING

THE BIG IDEA

Faith means believing in what seems to be impossible.

SESSION AIMS

In this session you will guide students to (1) understand that through faith, they can believe in the impossible; (2) realize that God knows that they have impossible situations in their lives; and (3) learn how to wait patiently for God to speak to them.

THE BIGGEST VERSE

"Is anything too hard for the LORD? I will return to you at the appointed time next year and Sarah will have a son" (Genesis 18:14).

OTHER IMPORTANT VERSES

Genesis 12:4; 15:3-6; 16:16; 17:1,15-16; 18:9-15; 21:1-7; 22:5; Exodus 33:14; Psalm 13; Jeremiah 29:11-13; Mark 9:23; Philippians 4:6-7; 1 Thessalonians 5:17; Hebrews 11:11-12; 1 Peter 5:7; 1 John 4:8

Note: Additional options and worksheets in 8^1/$_2$" x 11" format for this session are available for download at **www.gospellight.com/uncommon/jh_listening_to_God.zip**.

STARTER

Option 1: Push that Rock. For this option, you will need just this case study. Read the first part of the following story to the group members:

> One night as Joe was sleeping, his room suddenly filled with light, and Jesus appeared. Jesus took Joe outside and showed him a large rock. He explained that He wanted Joe to push against the rock with all his strength.
>
> So, for years, day after day, from sunup to sunset, Joe pushed on that cold and unmoving rock. Each evening, Joe returned home feeling worn out and discouraged. He felt that he was just wasting his time.
>
> Once when Joe seemed particularly discouraged, Satan appeared and said, "Joe, you haven't budged that rock yet, and you never will." Joe agreed that the task was impossible and that he was a failure.
>
> Joe considered pretending to push the rock, just to show enough effort to look as if he were trying. But first he decided to pray. "Jesus, I've worked long and hard," he said, "and I've put all my strength into what You asked me to do. But I haven't been able to move the rock. Why am I failing?"

At this point, discuss the following questions:

- Should Joe continue to push or should he give up?
- Do you think Joe will ever move the rock?
- Have you ever felt as if God were asking you to do something that was impossible?
- If so, how did you deal with it?

Now continue the story:

> Jesus responded compassionately, saying, "Joe, I asked you to push against the rock with all your strength. You did that, and now you feel tired and as if you are a failure. But look at yourself. You have strong muscles in your arms and your back and your legs. Your hands have calluses from the pressure. Because of the rock's resistance, you have grown considerably stronger. I didn't say that I expected you to *move* the rock. Your job was to obey me faithfully and to push. Now *I* will move it."

Discuss the following questions with the students:

- Do you think Jesus' response to Joe was helpful? Why or why not?
- Like Joe's hardened muscles, what spiritual results can we receive by faithfully obeying Jesus?
- Have you ever seen God do something that was humanly impossible? If so, what happened?

Explain that God can do things that are impossible by human standards. Often He asks us to participate in the process. As Joe learned, believing in Jesus and obeying His voice, even when it seems that what we have been asked to do is impossible, strengthens our faith.

Option 2: Bat that Balloon. For this option, you will need an oscillating fan, tape, paper bags and balloons. Ahead of time, decide whether you want the course for this activity to be straight, circular or curved. Use tape to mark the start and the finish lines of the course.

Welcome the group members and distribute a paper bag and a balloon to each person. Instruct the group members to roll the bags into batons, and then have them blow up the balloons and tie them. (*Note:* If you have more than 15 students, you can choose volunteers to play the game and designate the rest of the group as the audience.)

Explain that the object of this game is to be the first person to cross the finish line with his or her balloon intact. Once the game begins, they must use their batons to keep their balloons in the air. They are not allowed to hold the balloons. If a balloon drops to the ground, the player must start over. Players can use their batons to hit other students' balloons out of their way as long as their balloons are still in the air.

Instruct the group members to line up at the starting line, and then turn on the fan so that it blows toward the course. (Slightly more than a gentle breeze should be enough to shake up the game. You may need to turn it up if players are reaching the finish line too easily.) Now start the game, and end when the first person crosses the finish line. Once the race is over, discuss the following questions:

- Did you feel like this game was impossible to win?
- What made it so hard?
- What else in your life seems impossible right now?

Share some examples with the group of impossible situations. Maybe they are in a class that they just can't understand or perhaps they don't agree with some of the choices their friends have made. Explain that it is easy to feel helpless. For the students, it is an impossible situation. However, God can do the impossible. Today the group is going to learn that faith means believing in what seems impossible.

MESSAGE

Option 1: Genealogy. For this option, you will need several Bibles and copies of "Genealogy" (found on the next two pages). Ahead of time, copy and cut out the cards on the handout.

Begin by explaining that today you will be telling the group about a man in the Bible named Abraham. Abraham was living in a place called Haran when he heard the voice of God telling him to take his family and move to a place that God would show him. God promised to make him into a great nation, even though Abraham and his wife were very old at the time and had no children. Abraham obeyed God's voice and set out for the land of Canaan.

Read Genesis 15:3-6. Explain that as the years went by, Abraham and his wife, Sarah, still did not have a child, and they grew impatient waiting for God's promise. So Sarah came up with a plan for her maidservant, Hagar, to have a son with Abraham. The boy born to Hagar was named Ishmael. However, what Sarah didn't realize is that she was an important part of God's promise. Read Genesis 17:15-16. Ishmael would *not* be the promised son that God would use to turn Abraham's descendants into a nation.

Continue by stating that Abraham and Sarah went back to waiting. Would the promised son ever arrive? Choose a student to read Genesis 18:9-15. Explain that in this scene, God appeared to the couple and told Abraham in person that Sarah would have a son. Note that when the Lord appeared to Abraham and Sarah, he was 99 and she was 89 years old (see Genesis 17:1; 21:5). This is

Youth Leader Tip
Give your students opportunities to grow in their leadership skills. Allow them to lead in prayer, write prayer requests on the board, help lead worship or operate sound and video equipment. Help them grow in confidence and mature in service a step at a time.

GENEALOGY

Isaac
Father: Abraham
Mother: Sarah

Simeon
Father: Jacob
Mother: Leah
Birth order: Jacob's second son

Esau
Father: Isaac
Mother: Rebekah
Birth order: You and Jacob are
    twins, so stand side by side.

Levi
Father: Jacob
Mother: Leah
Birth order: Jacob's third son

Jacob
Father: Isaac
Mother: Rebekah
Birth order: You and Esau are
    twins, so stand side by side.

Judah
Father: Jacob
Mother: Leah
Birth order: Jacob's fourth son

Reuben
Father: Jacob
Mother: Leah
Birth order: Jacob's first son.
    Stand right behind Jacob.

Dan
Father: Jacob
Mother: Bilhah
Birth order: Jacob's fifth son

Naphtali
Father: Jacob
Mother: Bilhah
Birth order: Jacob's sixth son

Dinah
Father: Jacob
Mother: Leah
Birth order: Jacob's daughter, born
after Zebulun

Gad
Father: Jacob
Mother: Zilpah
Birth order: Jacob's seventh son

Joseph
Father: Jacob
Mother: Rachel
Birth order: Jacob's eleventh son

Asher
Father: Jacob
Mother: Zilpah
Birth order: Jacob's eighth son

Manasseh
Father: Joseph
Mother: Asenath
Birth order: Joseph's oldest son.
Stand right behind Joseph.

Isaachar
Father: Jacob
Mother: Leah
Birth order: Jacob's ninth son

Ephraim
Father: Joseph
Mother: Asenath
Birth order: Joseph's second son.
Stand to the right of Manasseh.

Zebulun
Father: Jacob
Mother: Leah
Birth order: Jacob's tenth son

Benjamin
Father: Jacob
Mother: Rachel
Birth order: Jacob's twelfth son.
Stand right behind Manasseh.

why she laughed (though she lied about it).[1] God promised Abraham that Sarah would have a son one year later. But did this seemingly impossible promise come to pass? Did God make Abraham and Sarah into a mighty nation?

At this point, choose one student to stand at the front of the room. Give everyone else one of the "Genealogy" cards. Tell the group that the student standing at the front of the room represents Abraham. They will be forming a family tree to represent the descendants of Abraham so that they can see how God fulfilled His promise. Each card you handed out lists a descendant of Abraham in addition to his or her father's name. They will need to line up in order according to the information on their cards.

State that the person who has the "Isaac" card can come up to the front to start the process, as indeed, just as God had promised, Sarah gave birth to a son one year later. Point out that many of Abraham's descendants had more than one child, so they will need to line up in birth order as indicated on the cards. In addition, some of the cards give specific directions as to where to stand (indicated with an asterisk in the chart below). Use the following genealogy chart to help the group members get organized if they get stuck:

Abraham

Isaac

Esau and Jacob*

Reuben*

Simeon

Levi

Judah

Dan

Naphtali

Gad

Asher

Isaachar

Zebulun

Dinah

Joseph

Manasseh and Ephraim*

Benjamin*

As an option, you can also divide the students into smaller groups. Give each group a copy of the Genealogy cards and see which group can place the cards in the correct order first. You may want to reward the winning group.

When everyone has found his or her place in the family tree, read Hebrews 11:11-12. Ask the group members what they think Christmas dinner would look like with a family this large—and these represent only a few generations of Abraham's descendants! Even though Abraham and Sarah were too old to have a baby, God gave them a son because they believed He could and would do what He had promised. Even though it seemed impossible, Abraham and Sarah trusted in God's voice.

Option 2: The World's Oldest Mother. For this option, you will just need several Bibles.

Introduce this message by reading Genesis 18:9-15. Explain that God did the "impossible" in the lives of Abraham and Sarah by giving them a son because they were too old to have children of their own. Choose volunteers to look up the following passages: Genesis 12:4; 15:3-6; 16:16; 17:1,15-17; 22:5. When the volunteers have found their passages, have them read each of the verses in order.

Explain that in Genesis 12:4, we learn that Abraham was 75 years old when he heard God's voice and obeyed the Lord's command to go to Haran. The relationship between God and Abraham began at this time, and God promised to make his descendants into a great nation (see Genesis 12:1-2). Later, God again promised Abraham that he would have a son (see Genesis 15:3-6). Abraham was 86 years old when Hagar, Sarah's servant, gave birth to his son Ishmael (see Genesis 16:16). Abraham was 99 and Sarah was 89 when the Lord came to them and confirmed that He would give them a son of their own (see Genesis 17:1,15-17).

Instruct the group members to follow along as you read Genesis 18:9-15. Explain that several times in this passage we read that Abraham and Sarah were too old to have children. Giving birth was no longer a human possibility. In fact, even in our modern era, it has still not happened. The oldest mother currently on record is Rajo Devi Lohan, who, with the assistance of modern technology, gave birth to a daughter at the age of 70. That's 19 years younger than Sarah was when she had Isaac. What's more, Lohan's pregnancy put her health at risk.[2]

Continue by stating that we read in this passage that Sarah laughed when she overheard the Lord telling Abraham that she would have a son by the next year. Previously, Abraham had also laughed when told that he would have a son (see Genesis 17:17-19). In fact, Isaac's name means "he laughs." It's just human nature to laugh when we hear something we think is ridiculous. At this point, tell your own favorite story of a ridiculous event or use one of the following stupid criminal stories:

- Police in Oakland, California, spent two hours attempting to subdue a gunman who had barricaded himself inside his home. After firing 10 tear gas canisters, officers discovered that the man was standing outside right next to them. He was shouting to give himself up.

- An Illinois man, pretending to have a gun, kidnapped a motorist and forced him to drive to two different automated teller machines. The kidnapper then proceeded to withdraw money from his own bank account.

- Police in Los Angeles had good luck with a robbery suspect who just couldn't control himself during a lineup. When detectives asked each man in the lineup to repeat the words, "Give me all your money or I'll shoot," the man shouted, "That's not what I said!"

- A bank robber in Virginia Beach got a nasty surprise when a dye pack designed to mark stolen money exploded in his Fruit-of-the-Looms. The robber apparently stuffed the loot down the front of his pants as he was running out the door. "He was seen hopping and jumping around," said police spokesman Mike Carey. Police have the man's charred trousers in custody.

State that it may not sound much like faith when you read about Abraham and Sarah's reaction, but the good news is that even when our first response isn't the right one, God remains gracious. If any of us learned that God would fulfill our wildest dreams, but that it would take 75 years to see it happen, we might laugh as well. But Abraham and Sarah's laughter didn't change God's faithfulness to them.

Conclude by having a volunteer read Genesis 21:1-7. Explain that when the Lord asked Abraham, "Is anything too hard for the LORD?" (Genesis 18:14), Abraham and Sarah believed in what seemed impossible. God rewarded their faith by giving them their long-awaited son. We can hear the love and joy in Sarah's voice in Genesis 21:6-7. The answer to her question is that only God would have said to Abraham that Sarah would nurse children. No one else would have said it, because it was impossible. But because God said it, they believed it, and God did it.

DIG

Option 1: Dreams that Fly. For this option, you will need several Bibles, three small prizes, paper and pens or pencils. Ahead of time, practice your paper-airplane folding technique.

Give each group member a piece of paper, and slowly show them how to fold a paper airplane. Give them a minute or two to fold their own, and then explain that people have always wanted to fly. However, it is physically impossible for humans to fly. Humans don't have wings, feathers or the anatomy to fly the way that birds do. Because of this, people created airplanes in which to fly.

Ask the group members to write some of their dreams or goals on the inside of their airplanes. Ask them to also include some of their own "impossible" situations. (They don't need to write any names down if that helps them feel more secure.) Once this is complete, have the group members line up across your room. Ask them to throw their airplanes and see which plane flies the farthest. You can give a few prizes for the plane that goes the farthest, the plane that does the most loops, and the plane that did the biggest nosedive. Ask the students to retrieve their planes, and then discuss the following:

- What are some of your dreams and goals?
- Do some of these feel impossible?
- What other "impossible" situations do junior-highers face?
- What do you do when you face an "impossible" situation?
- What would you do if, like Sarah, your dreams seemed as if they would never come true?
- In what ways does trusting in God's promises help in these situations?

Ask the students to find 1 Peter 5:7 in their Bibles and write it on the wings of their airplanes. When they're done, explain that God cares about our impossible situations just as much as He cared about Abraham and Sarah's desire to have a baby. Even though He won't always give us what we want, He will al-

Youth Leader Tip

If you have students who are new to navigating the Bible, explain how the Bible is divided into books, chapters and verses and how to use the contents page. Provide time for them to find passages for themselves, and encourage them to read along with you.

ways honor our willingness to trust in Him and obey His voice. When we do, who knows? Maybe God will make some of our impossible dreams fly.

Option 2: Possible Impossibilities. For this option, you will need several Bibles. Share the following case study with the group:

> Kristin watched in disbelief as Nicole walked away with Cece. Kristin and Nicole had been friends since birth. Seriously. Their moms met while they were both pregnant, and the girls grew up together. But recently, Nicole's attitude had changed. It started with her getting a bad grade on an English test she had studied really hard for. Nicole reasoned to herself, *If I get bad grades when I study, I might as well forget it and save myself the time!* Kristin tried to encourage her not to give up, but Nicole didn't listen.
>
> Next, Nicole stopped calling. The two used to talk every Tuesday night while they watched their favorite TV show. At first, Kristin thought that Nicole must have just forgotten to call, but when Nicole didn't return any of her messages, she became suspicious.
>
> One day at school, Kristin thought she saw Nicole talking to Cece. Kristin knew that Cece liked to talk about drinking. When she asked Nicole about it, Nicole said she hardly knew Cece and couldn't remember talking to her.
>
> But when they "bumped" into Cece at the mall, Kristin knew Nicole was lying. Nicole had arranged to go to the mall with Kristin as a cover story for their moms. Then she had arranged to meet Cece there and to ditch Kristin. Nicole casually said, "You can come if you want, Kristin." Kristin emphatically replied, "For a drink? No thanks. At least I know better. You should, too."

Discuss the following questions with the group:

- How do you think Kristin felt when she found out Nicole had been lying?
- Have you ever been in Kristin's position?
- What can you do about a friend who's obviously making poor choices?
- What does faith and obeying God have to do with our friendships?

Explain that God cares about us, our friends and our situations. When we have faith in God, He can take care of the "impossibilities." Choose a student to read Philippians 4:6-7. State that in the same way God cared about Abraham and Sarah's desire to have a baby, God cares about the things in our lives that seem impossible. Paul tells us in Philippians that we can pray in faith about anything that makes us feel anxious and God will give us peace.

APPLY

Option 1: Psalm 13. For this option, you will need several Bibles, copies of "Psalm 13" (found on the next page), and pens or pencils.

Distribute the Bibles, "Psalm 13" and pens or pencils. Explain that sometimes the hardest part of believing in what God has said is waiting for Him to act, especially if we're not sure He will do the thing we have asked. David, the author of Psalm 13, well understood that feeling and wrote prayers about it.

Ask the students to read Psalm 13 and then write down their own prayer to God about an impossible situation in their lives. They can copy the way the prayer is written in the psalm or use their own style. An example would be, "How long will I have to wait to make the pro baseball team?"

After a few minutes, choose a few volunteers to share their psalms. Close in prayer, asking God to strengthen the students' faith as they wait for Him to achieve what seems "impossible" in their lives. Remind students to take their psalms with them and to keep praying as they faithfully wait for God to act.

Option 2: Hidden Surprise. For this option, you will need several Bibles, permanent markers, plastic spoons, napkins, tapioca pudding (enough for each student to have a small cup), and a bag of white-chocolate chips. (Option: Use regular chocolate chips and chocolate pudding.) Ahead of time, put one white-chocolate chip in each cup of pudding. Stir up the pudding until the chip has been hidden. (Make sure the pudding is cold so that it does not melt the chip.)

Give each student a napkin, spoon and a cup of pudding. Explain that each cup of pudding holds a surprise they will find as they eat it. Let the group members eat their pudding, and tell them that when they think they have found the surprise, they should put it in their napkins instead of eating it right away. After everyone has found his or her surprise, invite the group to eat the chocolate chips. Then ask the following questions:

- What did you need to do to find the surprise? (*Eat the pudding.*)
- Was it possible to find the surprise if you had decided to throw the pudding away without eating it? (*No.*)

Psalm 13

Psalm 13	Your Letter to God
Verses 1-2: "How long, O LORD? Will you for-get me forever? How long will you hide your face from me? How long must I wrestle with my thoughts and every day have sorrow in my heart? How long will my enemy triumph over me?"	Tell God how you feel about your impossible situation.
Verses 3-4: "Look on me and answer, O LORD my God. Give light to my eyes, or I will sleep in death; my enemy will say, 'I have overcome him,' and my foes will rejoice when I fall."	Ask God to work in this situation.
Verses 5-6: "But I trust in your unfailing love; my heart rejoices in your salvation. I will sing to the LORD, for he has been good to me."	Tell God you will obey His voice and trust in Him.

Distribute Bibles and choose a volunteer to read Jeremiah 29:11-13. Explain that some of the group members may feel that believing in God is impossible. They also may feel that their prayers only hit the ceiling and not the ears of God. However, God promises that if we seek Him with all our hearts, we will find Him. He is the chocolate chip in the cup of pudding. We may have to look for Him for a while before we find Him—much in the same way they had to eat several bites of pudding before they found their chocolate chips—but God promises that if we keep listening for His voice, we will hear it. It's up to us to then act on what He says.

Distribute the permanent markers. Invite the students to write "God" on their spoons if during the next week they are willing to seek God. They can take their spoons home with them as a reminder to keep seeking God and to wait patiently for Him and His good plans. End in prayer, thanking the Lord for His promises and asking Him to reveal Himself to each student in the group in His perfect timing.

REFLECT

The following short devotions are for the students to reflect on and answer during the week. You can make a copy of these pages and distribute to your class or download and print from **www.gospellight.com/uncommon/jh_listening_to_God.zip.**

1—YOU CAN DO IT!

Worried? Anxious? Then read God's words to you in Exodus 33:14.

Tim and Dave were really nervous and really excited. It was their first mission trip to Mexico, where they would be working with a team on the construction of a house.

The drive to Mexico had taken longer than either of them had expected. By the time they arrived, it was pitch black outside. What they could see of the village where they would be staying was a little scary. There was no electricity or running water. The "houses" the villagers lived in were little more than cardboard shacks. The people in the village all looked at the church vans as if they were transporting aliens from another planet, and not necessarily friendly aliens either.

Before bed, the leader of the building project told them what they would be working on in the next week. It sounded like more work than either of them had ever done before in their entire lives.

"Do you think that was really a good idea?" Tim whispered to Dave. "Seems like what they are asking us to do in a week is impossible."

How would you answer Tim?

_____

_____

_____

_____

Have you ever faced a situation that seemed impossible to you? If so, what did you do?

_____

_____

_____

_____

God promises to take care of you, even when what you're doing is really hard. He knows exactly what's going on, and He wants to help you through any situation, even if it seems impossible. Spend at least 10 minutes with Him right now.

2—YES, YOU CAN

Facing a tough situation and ready to give up? Then check out Mark 9:23.

Imagine your mom is going to pay you to do a few things around the house. She gives you a list. Place a check mark in the box next to the things you think you could do.

- ❑ Clean up the kitchen
- ❑ Wash the car
- ❑ Take out the trash
- ❑ Walk the dog
- ❑ Wash the windows
- ❑ Pick the house up and move it three blocks to Elm Street

In Mark 9:23, what does God say is possible for those who believe in Him?

_____

_____

_____

_____

Do you truly believe this? Why or why not?

_____

_____

_____

_____

God tells us that *nothing* is impossible if we have faith and obey His voice. What seems impossible to you? Maybe you have a friend who is sick, and you are afraid he or she will never get better. Maybe there is something you need, but you feel you will never get it. Right now, give whatever seems impossible in your life to God and have faith. God will take care of you.

3—SOME THINGS TAKE TIME

How are we to pray? Go find 1 Thessalonians 5:17.

Dana isn't what you might call the most patient person in the world. She's the type of girl who opens the microwave door about a million times when making a burrito. She'll leave nine messages on your answering machine, one right after the other, asking, "Where are you? What's taking you so long?" When she prays, it's the same thing. If God doesn't answer her prayer in nanoseconds, she gives up.

What does Paul say about this in 1 Thessalonians 5:17?

_____

_____

_____

_____

Part of having faith is understanding that we need to wait and be patient. Many times, we think God needs to act *right now* in order to help us, but that just isn't the way it works. Do you ever act like Dana and give up on God because it just isn't going fast enough for you? If so, how?

_____

_____

_____

_____

How can you help yourself remember to wait patiently for God today?

_____

_____

_____

_____

4—KEEP ON KEEPING ON

There's a garage sale going on down the street. Check out some of the items that they have for sale:

- ❑ A half-built doghouse ($5)
- ❑ A partially knitted sweater, a messy pile of yarn and some knitting needles ($2)
- ❑ A neat looking lamp, half-broken ($4)
- ❑ A half-assembled bicycle ($20)
- ❑ Scrumptious half-baked brownies! (50 cents)

Have you ever started a project but then didn't finish it? If so, what was it, and what stopped you from completing it?

_____

_____

_____

_____

Why do people give up tasks when they are halfway through them?

_____

_____

_____

While we might start things that we don't finish, God isn't like that. You can trust that when you're working with God, He will be there to help you finish whatever it is you're doing. Think about one thing in your life that God is still working on. Pray about that area today, and make sure you thank Him for what He's up to!

OBEYING GOD'S VOICE AND WALKING IN FAITH

THE BIG IDEA

Obeying God's voice and walking in faith means seeing the opportunities that God sets in front of us and doing something with them.

SESSION AIMS

In this session, you will guide students to (1) understand that God gives them opportunities to hear His voice and grow their faith; (2) feel challenged to keep their eyes open to opportunities from God; and (3) commit to one new step of faith this week.

THE BIGGEST VERSE

"By faith the people passed through the Red Sea as on dry land; but when the Egyptians tried to do so, they were drowned" (Hebrews 11:29).

OTHER IMPORTANT VERSES

Exodus 14:5-31; Leviticus 20:26; Psalm 119:105; Proverbs 12:15; Isaiah 41:9-10; Matthew 22:37-40; 28:18-20; Mark 11:24; Hebrews 11:29; James 1:17; 1 Peter 3:15

Note: Additional options and worksheets in 8^1/$_2$" x 11" format for this session are available for download at **www.gospellight.com/uncommon/jh_listening_to_God.zip**.

STARTER

Option 1: Tug-o-War Switch. For this option, you will need a long, sturdy rope, a piece of masking tape and lots of space! Ahead of time, use the tape to make a middle line in the game area.

Greet the group members and divide them into two teams for a game of Tug-o-War. Each team must try to pull the other team across the middle line to their side. No big deal, right? Ah, but this game has an added twist. After a minute or so of play, yell "switch sides." The teams must stop exactly where they are, drop the rope and—you guessed it—switch sides! This should add some chaos as students rush to grab the opposite end of the rope so they can pull it and the other team over to their side before their opponents can.

Start the game. After a minute of play, signal for the teams to switch. After another minute of play, signal for them to switch again, and so on until one team is able to pull the other team across the line and to their side. Declare that team the winners of the game. (*Note*: A good game of Tug-o-War is fun, but it can be hazardous without one significant ground rule—students cannot wrap the rope around their arms, hands or *any* other body part.)

Ask the group members why they think the winning group succeeded. (The answer would be that the members were stronger and more powerful.) Explain that there are many forces that are even more powerful than the strongest team. *The* most powerful force in existence is God. Today, the group will be hearing a story from the Bible about God using His power to give the Israelites a faith-growing lesson.

Option 2: Power Surge. For this option, you will need a flashlight. Ahead of time, place the flashlight on a chair in the game area.

Greet the group members and ask the students who like creamy peanut butter the best to go to the left side of the room. They will be Team 1. Have those who like chunky peanut butter the best go to the right side of the room. They will be Team 2. If the teams are uneven, even them up. Each team should stand facing the opposite team, and each team member must hold the hand of the person on either side of him or her. The team members' hands must also be hidden behind them so that the other team cannot see them. The first person from each team should hold your hand. Put the flashlight on a chair in front of you.

Explain that you will pass a power surge to the first person on each team by squeezing his or her hand. Once that player's hand gets squeezed, he or she must pass the power surge to the next person by squeezing his or her hand.

This process needs to keep going until the power surge reaches the last person in line. Once the last person receives the power surge, he or she can run forward to grab the flashlight. The person who grabs the flashlight first wins that round and gets to be the first in line. The losing team maintains the same positions. The first team to rotate through all its members wins.

When the game is over, explain that if this had been a real power surge, we might have all died from touching it. Power is just that—*powerful*. However, God's power is even greater. When the person at the end of the line felt the power surge, he or she had to respond quickly. That is how it is with God. When He speaks to us and displays His power by providing opportunities for us to follow, we need to respond. As we will learn today, faith means being a part of the opportunities that God provides.

MESSAGE

Option 1: The Getaway. For this option, you will need copies of "The Getaway" script (found on the next page).

Tell the group members that they will be acting out a story found in Exodus 14:5-31. The point of this drama is to show that part of obeying God's voice means taking hold of the opportunities He puts before us. Pass out copies of "The Getaway" and assign the following parts: Moses (one person), the Red Sea (at least two people), the Israelites (at least two people), and the Egyptians (at least two people). You might want to assign a few more Egyptians than Israelites to demonstrate the strength of the Egyptian army.

Ask the student actors to line up as follows: (1) the Red Sea, (2) Moses, (3) the Israelites, and (4) the Egyptians. Have the group members act out the motions or say the appropriate lines as you read the script. You will need to pause occasionally to allow them to do so. In order to keep the action moving while you narrate, you might want to have the Israelites walk around on one side of the sea while the Egyptians walk around on the other side of the sea.

Youth Leader Tip
Encourage students to ham it up during the scene. The Israelites can shriek in fear while the Egyptians can shout menacingly. The more enthusiasm they give to their parts, the more fun this activity will be.

The Getaway

Based on Exodus 14:21-31

Cast

Moses	The Israelites
The Red Sea	The Egyptians

The Scene

Then Moses stretched out his hand over the sea (MOSES, STRETCH OUT YOUR ARM), and all that night the Lord drove the sea back (SEA, PART IN TWO AND HOLD YOUR ARMS UP OVER YOUR HEADS) with a strong east wind and turned it into dry land. The waters divided, and the Israelites went through the sea on dry ground (ISRAELITES, START WALKING), with a wall of water on their right and on their left.

The Egyptians pursued them (EGYPTIANS, LOUDLY PURSUE THE ISRAELITES INTO THE SEA), and all Pharaoh's horses and chariots and horsemen followed them into the sea. During the last watch of the night, the Lord looked down from a pillar of fire and cloud at the Egyptian army and threw it into confusion (EGYPTIANS, ACT CONFUSED). He made the wheels of their chariots come off so they had difficulty driving. And the Egyptians said (EGYPTIANS, REPEAT AFTER THE NARRATOR), "Let's get away from the Israelites! The Lord is fighting for them against Egypt." (ISRAELITES, FINISH CROSSING THE SEA.)

Then the Lord said to Moses, "Stretch out your hand over the sea so that the waters may flow back over the Egyptians and their chariots and horsemen." Moses stretched out his hand over the sea (MOSES, STRETCH OUT YOUR HAND), and at daybreak the sea went back to its place (SEA, SCOOT IN AND JOIN HANDS OVER THE EGYPTIANS). The Egyptians were fleeing, and the Lord swept them into the sea (EGYPTIANS, ACT PANICKED AND LET THE SEA SQUISH YOU IN AND CLOSE OVER YOUR HEADS). The water flowed back and covered the chariots and horsemen—the entire army of Pharaoh that had followed the Israelites into the sea. Not one of them survived.

But the Israelites went through the sea on dry ground, with a wall of water on their right and on their left. That day the Lord saved Israel from the hands of the Egyptians, and Israel saw the Egyptians lying dead on the shore (EGYPTIANS, LIE DEAD ON THE SHORE. ISRAELITES, LOOK AT THE DEAD EGYPTIANS). And when the Israelites saw the great power the Lord displayed against the Egyptians, the people feared the Lord (ISRAELITES, KNEEL IN AWE OF GOD) and put their trust in Him and in Moses His servant.

Set up the scene by stating that the Israelites, God's people, were slaves in Egypt. When they cried out to God for freedom, the Lord sent Moses to talk to the king of Egypt (Pharaoh) and tell him to let the Israelites go. When Pharaoh refused, God sent 10 plagues against the Egyptians. The final plague involved an angel of death taking the life of the firstborn in every household. The Israelites were spared because God had told them to put the blood of a lamb on their doorposts, so the angel would "pass over" their houses. After this plague hit Pharaoh's household, he told Moses to take the people and leave. But once they were gone, Pharaoh started having second thoughts.

Read the script and have the group members act out the appropriate parts. After the drama is over, discuss the following questions:

- What opportunity did God give to the Israelites? (*The chance to escape the Egyptians by crossing the Red Sea [Exodus 14:21-22].*)
- Why did the Israelites need to obey God's voice? (*So they would be able to walk down into the parted sea.*)
- How did they demonstrate their faith in God? (*They went through the sea [verse 22]!*).
- How did God demonstrate His power? (*All sorts of ways. He parted the sea and dried the ground [verse 21]; He confused the Egyptians [verse 24]; He jammed the Egyptian's chariot wheels [verse 25]; He spoke to Moses [verse 26]; He swept the sea over the Egyptians [verse 27]; He destroyed the entire Egyptian army [verse 28]; He saved Israel from the Egyptians [verse 30].*)
- What would have happened to the Israelites if they hadn't obeyed God's voice? (*They wouldn't have entered the Red Sea, and the Egyptians would have killed them.*)
- How did the Israelites' faith change as a result of seeing God's power at work? (*They were amazed at the Lord's power and trusted in Him [verse 31]. Their faith grew because they saw what God could do.*)

Explain that God provided a way out for the Israelites, but they still had to take that first scary step and walk out into the Red Sea. They had to believe that God would keep the waters parted long enough for them to get through. If they hadn't had faith, they might not have entered the sea at all, and that would have meant certain destruction. Faith means taking hold of the opportunities God puts in front of us.[1]

Option 2: Ping-Pong Catch. For this option, you will need several Bibles and one Ping-Pong ball for every two students.

Explain to the group that faith means following God's voice and taking hold of the opportunities He gives to us. However, in order to exercise faith, we need to be able to recognize God's voice in our lives. After all, God is always working around us. If we have faith, we can respond to what He is doing.

Ask the group members to close their eyes and try to imagine the story of the Israelites' escape across the Red Sea as you read Exodus 14:21-31 and Hebrews 11:29. Explain that they will be examining the Red Sea story from the perspective of the two groups of people who are involved—the Egyptians and the Israelites—in order to see that God's power works for those who believe in Him and follow His voice.

Choose a volunteer to read Exodus 14:23. Explain that this story comes at the end of a long debate between Moses (as the representative of God) and Pharaoh (as the representative of Egypt). Pharaoh refused to recognize God and His power, even though God did tremendous miracles that hurt Egypt. Pharaoh was concerned with his own power and Egypt's power rather than God. As a result, the Egyptians had their eyes on the Israelites, not on God.

Pair up the students and give each pair one ping-pong ball. Explain that the partners are going to play catch, but there is a twist (of course): the partner in each pair *not* holding the ball is going to look down at his or her feet (yes, *actually* look down) while trying to catch the ball thrown by his or her partner. Instruct partners to move approximately six feet apart, and then give the signal to toss the balls. After a couple of tries, have the partners switch so that each one gets to try to catch the ball while looking at his or her toes.

Explain that while some of the players probably caught the ball, they didn't do so as effortlessly as they might have if they had their focus in the right place. The Egyptians had their focus in the wrong place. They entered the parted sea in vengeance, not in faith. While they were in the midst of it, the Egyptian army recognized God's power at work, but they didn't have faith in Him. Because

they set themselves against God and His people, God wiped them out. Sure, they experienced God's power, but they didn't benefit from it.

Choose three volunteers to come to the front, and have them stand with their shoulders touching. Invite the two on the outside to lean in (but not crush the one in the middle) and hold their positions. Explain that the Israelites found themselves squeezed between a rock and a hard place: an impassable sea and an army. They were seriously stuck. Nothing they could do would change their situation. When they expressed their fear to Moses, he replied, "Do not be afraid. Stand firm and you will see the deliverance the LORD will bring you today. The Egyptians you see today you will never see again. The LORD will fight for you; you need only to be still" (Exodus 14:13-14). Because the Israelites stood firm and believed what God said, they were able to cross the Red Sea on dry ground.

Ask one of the outside volunteers to slowly—so as not to make everyone fall down—move out of the way. Explain that the Israelites had a way out because of God's power. They recognized God at work and obeyed His voice.

Ask the group members to share some situations in which they feel helpless. Explain that God cares about their difficult situations, and, like the Israelites, He will fight for them. They just need to have faith and recognize the opportunities that God gives to them. When the Israelites entered the sea, they took refuge in God because of their faith. God is powerful, and He is at work all around us. It is up to us to recognize what He is asking us to do and have the faith to do it.

DIG

Option 1: An Offer You Can't Refuse. For this option, you will need several Bibles and a piece of junk mail (you know, the kind promising the one-time-only-never-to-be-offered-again incredible deal).

Show the group members the junk mail and tell them about the amazing opportunity it promises. Invite them to share similar memorable advertisements they have seen. Ask if they think it would be helpful if God spelled out what He was offering in clear, large type like in this piece of junk mail. Wouldn't it be nice if God sent us a letter that told us in simple steps what He wanted us to do today, this week or even for the next 50 years?

Now discuss the following questions with the group:

- How do you recognize the opportunities that God brings into your life?
- Have you ever heard God speak and know that the opportunity in front of you was from God? If so, how did you know?

- If you have two options that both seem to be good, how do you decide which one God wants you to do?

Choose three volunteers to read Psalm 119:105, Proverbs 12:15 and Mark 11:24. Discuss the following questions:

- How can the Bible, wise advice from another Christian and prayer help you recognize an opportunity from God?
- What would you do if you had an opportunity that agreed with what the Bible said and you didn't hear God tell you not to do it, but your parents were against it?

Explain that sometimes recognizing the opportunities God gives us can be tricky. Other times they will be a no-brainer. God may not send us individual instructions that are quite as clear as the ones in the junk mail, but God's instructions are there—and they are always more reliable and true. He has sent us help in the form of the Bible, prayer and advice from wise Christian people.

Option 2: Ben's Choice. For this option, you will need mosquito repellent and poster paint to illustrate Ben's options. Share the following case study:

Ben has a decision to make. He could spend next week camping with a friend's family or help out with his church's Vacation Bible School (VBS) program. He's disappointed that he can't do both. The rest of his summer has been kind of slow. Now he has two great opportunities in one week.

On one hand, the camping trip would be relaxing. He knows he would enjoy fishing with his friend Jon and Jon's dad. Jon also mentioned some great hiking trails. And, somehow, food always tastes better when Ben gets to eat outside. Plus there would be a campfire every night.

On the other hand, Ben has been volunteering in the second-grade Sunday School class all year. He enjoys playing with the children and helping them do crafts that teach them about Jesus. The teacher, Mrs. Phillips, had asked him to help her during VBS. They really need the extra help since they expect neighborhood children to attend as well.

Ben wants to do what God wants him to do, but he doesn't know what that is.

Hold up the mosquito repellent and tell the group members that it stands for the camping trip. Ask them to cheer if they think Ben should choose the camping trip. Now hold up the poster paint and tell them it stands for helping at VBS. Ask the students to cheer if they think Ben should choose helping at VBS. After the vote, discuss the following questions:

- If Ben came to you for advice, what would you say?
- Have you ever been in a situation like Ben's? If so, what did you do?
- Is the VBS option necessarily what God wants just because it's church-related?
- Is the camping option necessarily what God doesn't want just because it's fun?
- How could the Bible, prayer and advice from other wise Christians help Ben recognize which opportunity God wants him to take?

Explain that opportunities that come from God don't always look like church activities. It could be that instead of a church-sponsored VBS, God wants Ben to be a good friend to Jon. Maybe Ben needs a break from service and a chance to relax. The other side would be that even though Ben might prefer camping, God may want him to make the harder decision and faithfully serve Him at VBS. Either way, Ben will be able to understand much better what God wants him to do as he spends time reading the Bible, praying and asking other wise Christians for advice.

APPLY

Option 1: Stuck on the Shore? For this option, you will need index cards and pens or pencils.

Distribute the index cards and pens or pencils to the group members. Explain that when the Israelites came up to the Red Sea, they had to make a choice. One choice was for them to follow God's command and step out in faith. The other choice was to allow the Egyptians to capture them and take them back as slaves.

Ask the group to think about the following questions:

- You probably are not running from an army, nor are you in danger of becoming a slave (and, no, household chores don't count as slavery). However, do fear and difficult situations in your life keep you from doing the things that God is calling you to do?

- Are you stuck on the shore, unable to move forward because you are uncertain what a life of following God will mean for you?
- Are you unwilling to give up the way you live now?
- Will you take a risk to follow where God is trying to lead you?

Allow students to sit with these questions for a few minutes, and then ask them to write down on their index cards one way that they would like to take a step of faith this week. Have them take the cards home and put them in a place where they will see them each day as a reminder of the commitment they have made. Close by praying that God will help the group members know what He wants them to do and to rely on His power and support to do it.

Option 2: Super-size It. For this option, you will need several Bibles, pens or pencils and napkins or paper bags imprinted with the McDonald's logo. (Be sure to ask the manager on duty before you go taking a whole stack of napkins!)

Explain that when you go to McDonald's, you have the opportunity to super-size your meal. For just a few cents more, you can add an extra amount of soda and fries. This seems like a pretty good deal. In the same way, when you faithfully follow God and obey His voice, you have the opportunity to super-size your faith. This is a truly great deal.

Have the group members silently read Matthew 22:37-40 and Matthew 28:18-20. When they have been reading for a few minutes, ask them to think about one thing they could do this week that might be an opportunity from God. For example, God might want them to show love to their elderly next-door neighbor by volunteering to walk her dog.

Tell the group members that when they have an idea, they should come forward and get a pen and a McDonald's napkin/bag. They will write their idea under the flap of the napkin or on the bag and then fold it over the idea. Have them take their napkins/bags with them as a reminder to super-size their faith by taking hold of the opportunities God gives to them each day.

Youth Leader Tip

Watch for students who may need help in thinking about what God might want them to do. Talk with them about how they can practice living out God's commands to help ground them in the reality of a personal God.

REFLECT

The following short devotions are for the students to reflect on and answer during the week. You can make a copy of these pages and distribute to your class or download and print from **www.gospellight.com/uncommon/jh_listening_to_God.zip.**

1—HUH?

Andrew is what you call *oblivious*. He never pays attention to what is going on around him. He never looks before crossing the street. He never answers the door or the phone, because he never hears the ring. He runs into people in the halls and trips all the time because he is, as we said, oblivious.

On Sunday, Andrew's pastor gave a sermon about the opportunities to serve God that are all around us every day. *Huh?* Andrew thought. *Opportunities? What's he talkin' about? I never see any opportunities.*

How would you respond if you were a friend of Andrew's?

_____

_____

_____

Are you ever guilty of being like Andrew? Do you have trouble seeing the opportunities God gives to you every day?

_____

_____

_____

_____

Today, ask God to make you aware of opportunities He has put right in front of you to serve Him today.

2—YOUR UNIFORM

Pop quiz! Okay, you don't need a pencil, just answer these easy questions in your head:

1. What kind of uniform does a police officer wear?
2. How do lawyers dress to go to court?

3. What kind of outfit does a clown wear?
4. How can you tell the queen of England apart from other people (think of her *head*).

Read Leviticus 20:26. What does God tell us we are to be?

_____

_____

_____

_____

The word "holy" in this verse really means "set apart." In what way have you been set apart by God?

_____

_____

_____

_____

When other people look at you, do they see that you are a follower of Jesus Christ by the way that you live your life and by what you do? Why or why not?

_____

_____

_____

_____

Your behavior is like a uniform you wear. It will tell others that what you are doing is for God. What's one way you can let people know that you're working for God today?

_____

_____

_____

_____

3—A CASE OF THE JITTERS

Have no fear and read Isaiah 41:9-10.

Michelle was nervous. It was her first night as a volunteer at the Grace Rescue Center. Her cousin had worked there for years and had encouraged

Michelle to come down and help. Earlier that night when she was getting ready to go, it had sounded exciting. But now that Michelle was standing at the beginning of the food line, she was nervous.

Michelle's job was to give a tray and eating utensils to the hungry men and women who were lining up to be fed. But her hands were shaking so badly that she was afraid she would drop the trays or the utensils all over the floor.

What could Michelle gain from reading Isaiah 41:9-10 right now?

_____

_____

_____

_____

Even though Michelle has a case of the jitters, it's pretty cool that she's still going through with the volunteer job. Serving God can mean being uncomfortable sometimes, but it is important that you do serve. Is there something you think God might want you to start doing that scares you a bit when you think about it?

_____

_____

_____

_____

What does God promise that He will do when you obey what He has told you to do?

_____

_____

_____

_____

Today, ask God for the strength and courage to always obey His voice.

4—WHAT'S IN A NAME?

We've all seen the bracelets, the T-shirts and even the coffee mugs with the "Christianese" initials on them. You know the ones—there's WWJD for "What Would Jesus Do," and FROG for "Fully Rely On God," and a whole bunch of others. But I bet you've never seen anyone wearing wristbands with these initials on them:

- SLUG: "Sorry, Lord, Unable to Give"
- TANIB: "Take A Number, I'm Busy"
- PASE: "Please Ask Someone Else"
- SIBN: "Sounds Interesting, But No"

Can you imagine wearing one of these bracelets? Maybe not, but there are probably times when you've wanted to say something like that to God—such as when He has asked you to do something that seems difficult or scary. Today, pray that God will help your attitude to be one that's ready to serve Him.

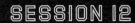

OBEYING GOD'S VOICE AT ALL TIMES

THE BIG IDEA

Faith means trusting in God's voice even when the circumstances in your life seem to be against you.

SESSION AIMS

In this session, you will guide students to (1) understand that God can be trusted in all circumstances; (2) feel encouraged to trust God even when everything seems to be going against them; and (3) pray and worship God because of His trustworthiness.

THE BIGGEST VERSE

"The LORD said to Gideon, 'With the three hundred men that lapped I will save you and give the Midianites into your hands. Let all the others go home'" (Judges 7:7).

OTHER IMPORTANT VERSES

Genesis 12:3; 18:9-15; 28:14; Exodus 14:21-31; Judges 7:1-25; Psalms 95:1-2; 139:13-16; Proverbs 3:5-6; Isaiah 41:10; Mark 9:14-29; Romans 5:8; 1 Corinthians 12; 2 Corinthians 12:9; Ephesians 2:1-10; Philippians 4:4-7; Colossians 3:17; 2 Timothy 3:16-17; Hebrews 11:32-34; James 2:14-19

Note: Additional options and worksheets in 8¹/₂" x 11" format for this session are available for download at **www.gospellight.com/uncommon/jh_listening_to_God.zip**.

STARTER

Option 1: The Worst Day. For this option, you will need some paper and pencils. Greet the group members and divide them into smaller groups of five to eight. Give each group paper and pencils. Ask the students how many of them have had a bad day, and allow them to briefly respond. (You might want to share a few of your own mishaps from today as well.) Explain that they will be writing a list of all the bad things that could happen to a junior-higher. Encourage them to be creative and outlandish! After giving the groups three to five minutes to brainstorm, ask each to choose its five best ideas.

When this is finished, tell the groups that they will be acting out their five best ideas (or worst, given they're all bummers) before the whole group. Although not every person in the group needs to be involved in acting out every idea, everyone should be involved acting out *at least one* idea. The adults in the room will judge how well the groups act out the situations (if you don't have enough adult volunteers, you might want to invite some parents to come for this lesson). Each group can earn up to 1,000 points for the quality of its ideas, and each group can also earn up to 1,000 points for how well they act out the idea. A group can earn up to a grand total of 2,000 points.

Let each group act out their five ideas, and then declare a winning team. Gather your students back together and discuss the following questions:

- From the skits that you have just seen, what was the worst thing that could happen to a junior-higher?
- What is the toughest thing that has happened to you recently?
- What did you do? Looking back, what do you wish you had done in that circumstance?
- What do you think God wants you to do when bad things happen?

Explain that it is inevitable that we will have bad things happen to us. It's a part of life. But as believers in Jesus, we can still trust in God and obey His voice.

Youth Leader Tip

When it comes to teaching junior-highers, sometimes you have to say the same thing over and over again, in slightly different ways, for them to really get it. Take advantage of this option to review everything you've studied so far during this study.

Option 2: Stacked Against You. For this option, you will need cans, index cards, pens and masking tape.

Greet the group members and divide them into small groups based on their favorite brand of soda. Give each group a pile of cans. Explain that they will be competing to see which group can stack their cans the highest. Each can must touch at least two other cans. When you give the signal to end the game, their towers must remain standing and unsupported for at least 15 seconds. Start the game and give the groups one minute to stack their cans. Signal the end of the game and then announce the winners.

Give each group the index cards, pens and masking tape. Explain that their task is to be the first group to label each can with a different circumstance that might be stacked against a junior-higher. They will do this by writing the circumstance on one of the index cards and taping it to a can. (Some examples might be that they are too young to get a job or they are too short to reach their locker.) If the cans fall while they do this, they will have to rebuild their tower.

Conclude by asking the groups to share some of their ideas. Explain that sometimes it feels that no matter what we do, the circumstances are stacked against us. However, God always knows about our situations, and He cares. As we will learn today, faith means trusting in God and obeying His voice even when nothing else seems to be going our way.

MESSAGE

Option 1: Down, Up, Freeze. For this option, you will need Bibles, the song "Get Down" by Audio Adrenaline (available for download online) and a way to play it for your group. Ahead of time, listen to the song so you can judge the best place to pause it to force your students to freeze in different positions.

Choose a few volunteers to help you read Judges 7:1-25. After the reading, tell the group members that you will be playing a song. They are to move around the room as the song plays. When they hear the word "down," they must stoop down. When they hear the word "up," they can stand up again. When the music stops, they need to freeze wherever they are and hold their position.

Play "Get Down" until everyone has had a chance to stoop down and stand up a couple of times. Pause the song randomly. During each pause, read one of the following questions and let the group members respond:

- Gideon had an army of 32,000 men. But God sent 22,000 men home. How many men did Gideon have left? (*In case you haven't done much math since you were in junior high, that would be 10,000 [verses 2-3].*)

- Gideon had an army of 10,000 men. But God sent 9,700 men home. How many men did Gideon have left? (*300 [verses 3,5-6].*)

- Now Gideon had an army of 300 men. When the enemy, the Midianites, appeared, how did things look for Gideon? (*Pretty bleak [verse 12].*)

- Gideon's army held trumpets, empty jars and torches. What do you think most armies who are about to attack their enemies would have in their hands? (*Swords and shields [verse 16].*)

- How do you think you would have felt if you were in Gideon's army? How did the circumstances seem to be stacked against them? (*They were outnumbered and carried really unusual weapons.*)

- Gideon's army blew their trumpets, broke their jars and shouted, "A sword for the LORD and for Gideon!" The LORD caused the enemy soldiers to fight each other. What does that say about God's trustworthiness? (*As we do what God calls us to do and rely on Him, He will fight our battles for us [verse 20-22].*)[1]

Try to time your pauses so the group members will be able to stoop, stand and answer a few questions before the song ends. When it does, allow the students to freeze, and then ask them to be seated.

Explain that because of Gideon's circumstances—because his army had so few men and they had trumpets in their hands instead of weapons—we might have thought that his army was going to lose. However, because God is trustworthy, He saved them by defeating the Midianites. Because Gideon obeyed God's voice and the army had faith that God could deal with their circumstances, God did what they had no chance of doing.

Option 2: Eyewitness Account. For this option, you will need copies of "Eyewitness Account" (found on the next page), the movie *Indiana Jones and the Last Crusade,* and a way to show it to your group. Ahead of time, find the scene where Indiana Jones must reach the Holy Grail in order to ensure the survival of his father, Dr. Jones, who's been shot by Nazis. Have this scene ready to play for your group before the session begins.

Show the movie scene, and then discuss the following questions:

- How do you think Indy felt as he looked at the ravine?
- If you had been in his place, would you have been able to take that first step? Why or why not?

EYEWITNESS ACCOUNT

(Based on Judges 7)

I, Purah, servant of Gideon, do solemnly swear to tell the truth, the whole truth, and nothing but the truth, so help me God.

The Israelite army was 32,000 strong, but God told Gideon that he wouldn't deliver the Midianites into their hands. He didn't want us to boast in our own strength. God told Gideon to send away anyone who trembled with fear. So 22,000 men left, and 10,000 remained.

But God thought we still had too many men. So He told Gideon to take them down to the water. Those who put their tongues down to the river were to be sent home, but those who used their hands to bring the water to their mouths—the cautious ones—could stay. So Gideon sent away all but 300 men.

Gideon faithfully obeyed what God was telling him to do, even when it didn't make sense. He knew that 300 men couldn't defeat the locust-like swarm of the enemy that was coming against them. He was afraid, but he followed God anyway.

God knew how Gideon felt, so He sent Gideon and me down to the enemy camp in the dark of night. We arrived just in time to hear a fellow share a dream with his friend. The friend interpreted the dream to mean that God had given Gideon and the Israelites the victory over them.

So Gideon worshiped. Right there in the enemy camp, Gideon got on his knees and prayed to God, thanking and praising Him for revealing and confirming what He would do. Gideon took courage in God and charged back up to the Israelite camp. He got everyone out of bed and ready for battle.

Now, "ready for battle" didn't mean battle as normal. No. Instead of swords and shields, we had trumpets, jars and torches. But Gideon trusted God—so much so that he believed God would provide the victory. His faith caught on, and even with our small number and strange weapons, we stood our ground, shouting with all our strength, "A sword for the LORD and for Gideon!"

We didn't even have to move. We blew our trumpets, broke the jars and shouted, and God made the Midianites turn on themselves. God caused them to fight the battle for us! The Midianites fled out of camp toward the Jordan River, where others cut them off and killed their leaders.

That's how it happened. I, Purah, do swear that this is the truth, and you'll find it recorded in Judges 7.

Pass out copies of "Eyewitness Account," and then choose several students to each read a paragraph or two of the handout. Discuss the following questions:

- How do you think Gideon felt as he sent the first 22,000 soldiers home?
- How do you think he felt when he had to send all but 300 of his soldiers home?
- How were Gideon's and Indy's situations similar?
- If you had been in Gideon's place, would you have been able to send so many men home, knowing that your enemy had so many soldiers? Why or why not?
- Indy and Gideon both felt fear. Do you think fear is ever a good reason not to trust God? Why or why not?
- How did God show Gideon that He could be trusted?

Explain that God showed Gideon that He could be trusted by doing what the small Israelite army could not have done: defeat the Midianites. Gideon and the Israelites only had to follow God's voice and trust that He could and would defeat their enemy. If God can be trusted to defeat mighty armies, we can certainly trust Him with the circumstances of our lives.

DIG

Option 1: Lean on God. For this option, you will need a pair of crutches and some Bibles. (*Note*: If you can get several pairs of crutches, you can choose as many volunteers as you have pairs of crutches. You also can allow different people to have a chance to try walking with the crutches.)

Choose a group member to come to the front and grab a pair of crutches. Explain to this person that he or she has just broken an ankle and needs the crutches for support. Ask the student to tell you which ankle is broken and al-

Youth Leader Tip

You may have heard people criticize God or religion as a "crutch" for feeble-minded people. However, Proverbs 3:5-6 makes it clear that God intends for us to lean on Him. He designed it that way for our good!

low him or her to practice walking with the crutches. Tell the group to shout "lean!" if they see your volunteer put his or her broken foot on the floor.

Now ask the volunteer to stop moving but continue to stand with the support of the crutches. Discuss the following questions with the group:

- What purpose do the crutches serve for someone who needs them?
- What would happen if [volunteer's name] really had a broken ankle and I took away the crutches? Would [volunteer] be able to walk?
- How courageous might [volunteer] feel about walking if he or she didn't have the crutches?

Choose a volunteer to read Proverbs 3:5-6 while the others follow along. Continue the discussion by asking the following questions:

- What does this verse say about leaning? (*We should lean on God by trusting Him with all our heart.*)
- Why? (*Because God is the only one whom we can really trust.*)
- Sometimes people criticize Christianity by saying it's a "crutch" for weak people. Is that true? (*Well, actually, yes, it is. Our sin has made us weak, so we need to lean on God.*)
- How can leaning on God and trusting in Him give us courage? (*God will support us as long as we lean on Him. That makes us able to walk even if we don't understand where we are going.*)

Explain that God created us to lean on Him. Without Him, we are broken people, and we can't heal ourselves. Because we're broken, our own understanding is broken as well. If we lean on it, the result will be like leaning on a broken ankle—we'll fall (or at least not be able to walk very well). But if we lean on God by trusting in Him and acknowledging Him in everything we do, He will make us able to walk.

Option 2: A Big Move. For this option, you will need this book and a Bible. Read the following story to your students:

Chad lives in a small town in Iowa. Many of his friends live on farms. He enjoys spending weekends and summers working with them, helping out wherever he can. Planting and harvesting make sense to him. Last year on his birthday, a friend's dad let him drive a tractor.

Chad's family lives in a nice house, and they have a couple of pets—a rabbit and a cat—but they certainly aren't farmers. Chad's mom works for an insurance company. She recently found out that she's being transferred to Chicago, and his family will have to move there by next month. That means that Chad will have to leave his friends and start over at a new school mid-year. He can't even take his pets, because his family might have to rent an apartment before they can find a house.

Chad doesn't want to go. Why can't his mom turn down the job? Why can't he stay in Iowa? What if he doesn't make new friends in Chicago? What if he hates living in the city? Why does life have to be so unfair?

Chad knows that he should trust God, but he doesn't feel very trusting right now.

Discuss the following questions:

- Have you ever been in a situation where your family had to move like Chad's did?
- What could you say to encourage Chad? (*Allow students to answer.*)
- How might hearing the story of Gideon help Chad trust in God?

Explain that Gideon trusted God against incredible odds, and God provided the victory. If Chad trusts God and goes to Chicago, God will encourage him and help him fit in and make new friends. Besides, trusting God will help Chad's attitude—who wants to make friends with a grump?

Read 2 Corinthians 12:9. Ask the group members how this verse could apply to Gideon. How could it apply to Chad? God made Gideon weak by taking away most of his soldiers, and then God demonstrated His power. Chad feels weak because he'll be in a new city and school, but that's an opportunity for God to show Chad how much He loves him and cares about what he's going through.

Explain to the group that they will experience many situations that will make them feel weak. They may not like it, but as they trust in God, it will become an opportunity for God to speak into their lives, grow their faith and do amazing things they couldn't do on their own. They can be encouraged that if they have faith and follow God's voice, the times when they feel the weakest will be the times when they will most clearly see God's power at work.

APPLY

Option 1: Pray Now. For this option, you will need a long piece of butcher paper, pens, copies of "Pray Now" (found on the next page) and a Bible. Ahead of time, copy "Pray Now" and cut it into cards. You will also need to tape the piece of butcher paper to one of your walls and write the numbers from 1 to 15 approximately one foot apart to give students room to draw.

Read Philippians 4:4-7. Distribute a "Pray Now" card and a pen to several group members. Explain to the students who have the cards that they should go to the paper and find the number that corresponds to their card. Then they will need to draw a picture of what is on their card. Here's the catch: they will only have 20 seconds to do it. (Yes, you will get some pretty lame drawings, but that will add to the fun.) After the group members have finished drawing, review the pictures and explain what was written on their card that they were trying to depict (in some cases, you probably won't be able to tell).

Explain that the key in the Philippians passage is that we should not be anxious when things are going against us but should pray in faith and trust God to take care of things. Give students a few minutes to pray on their own about something that is causing them anxiety. Ask them to surrender that problem to God with gratitude in the same way that Paul did in the Bible.

Option 2: Worship in Hard Times. For this option, you will need Bibles, index cards and pens.

Ask the students to form groups of three to four people. Distribute one index card and a pen to each group. Instruct the group members to write one reason a junior-higher might not want to trust God. When groups have finished, ask them to pass their cards to another group. Have the groups write the reason they think they could faithfully worship God even in the midst of the circumstance that is written on that card. Remind them to use the information they learned today from Gideon's story.

After a minute, ask the groups to share what they discussed. Explain that Gideon worshiped God and then got up and led the Israelites in a faith experience. In the same way, as we worship God in *all* circumstances—no matter how bad—we will be prepared to bring others into God's presence as well. Other people will notice that we have been with God, and they will want to know why we are doing all right even though things aren't going our way.

Close by praying that the students will see every circumstance as an opportunity to worship God and follow His voice. Also pray that they will have opportunities to lead their friends into God's presence.

Pray Now

The Scoop from Paul in Philippians 4:4-7

---

1. Rejoice in the Lord always.

---

2. I will say it again: Rejoice!	*9.* Present your requests
3. Let your gentleness be evident to all.	*10.* To God.
4. The Lord is near.	*11.* And the peace of God,
5. Do not be anxious about anything,	*12.* Which transcends all understanding,
6. But in every situation,	*13.* Will guard your hearts
7. By prayer and petition,	*14.* And your minds
8. With thanksgiving,	*15.* In Christ Jesus.

REFLECT

The following short devotions are for the students to reflect on and answer during the week. You can make a copy of these pages and distribute to your class or download and print from **www.gospellight.com/uncommon/jh_listening_to_God.zip**.

1—SHOUT FOR JOY

Read Psalm 100 . . . don't worry, it's short!
    According to this psalm, what are we to do?

- ❑ Shout for joy to the Lord
- ❑ Worship God with gladness
- ❑ Enter His gates with thanksgiving
- ❑ Give thanks to Him and praise Him
- ❑ All of the above

When times are hard, do you try to do everything yourself? Where do you go for help?

_____

_____

_____

Why can you praise God even when things are tough?

_____

_____

_____

_____

Today, ask yourself if there is anything in your life that you're trying to do all by yourself. If so, turn it over to God in prayer. He wants to help!

2—IT IS GOOD

Hurry to Psalm 54:6-7 and see what's good.
    Ugh, what an all-around bad day. Peter thought it was maybe the worst day ever. He hadn't woken up when his alarm clock went off, and his mom had

to wake him up five minutes before he was supposed to leave for school. He made the bus late and everyone was ticked at him. At school, he got a paper back with a big C minus on it—after he'd worked really hard on it.

Worst of all, Jerry, the biggest (and meanest) kid in school, played keep-away with his Bible in the middle of the hallway in front of everyone, making him feel stupid for bringing it to school in the first place.

How can Peter be thankful to God even on a day like this?

_____

_____

_____

_____

How can Psalm 54:6-7 encourage him?

_____

_____

_____

_____

God wants you to trust Him, because He really does love you and care about you, even when it seems like nothing is going right. How can you remind yourself of this, even on the worst of days?

_____

_____

_____

_____

3—DON'T BE DECEIVED

Be a doer and read James 1:22.

Sue is sitting in church on Sunday when she hears her pastor say that the Bible teaches us to honor our parents. Her pastor goes on to explain what "honor" means, and Sue quickly realizes that he is saying we need to *obey* our parents. The problem is that Sue's parents have told her that they don't want her watching a certain show on TV that *everyone* at school watches.

Sue wants to obey her parents, but she doesn't agree with their decision. She has even figured out a way around it: her friend has clips of the show on

YouTube at her house that she lets Sue watch. Since she's *technically* not watching the show on TV, she's *technically* not disobeying her parents. But now, sitting in church, she's not so sure.

Is Sue right? What advice would you give to her?

_____

_____

_____

According to James 1:22, if Sue knows that the Bible says she is supposed to honor her parents, but she watches the show on YouTube anyway, what is she actually doing?

_____

_____

_____

_____

How can Sue obey God's voice (His Word) even when it's tough to do?

_____

_____

_____

_____

4—WHEN REACHING OUT GOES WRONG

How are we to love others? Read Romans 12:10 to find out.

Well, Allison's Monday had been very surprising. You see, last Friday at school, she had been in the girl's locker room when she heard someone crying. She looked around and found Karen, a new girl, crying on a bench in the back of the locker room. She was about to walk away, but then she felt God urging her to talk to Karen. So Allison approached her.

"Are you okay?" she asked.

"Go away, church girl!" Karen said. "I don't need any of your preachy garbage!"

Ouch. Allison mumbled something and walked away. She felt lousy for almost the entire weekend and thought about Karen a lot. *Does she really think I don't care?* she said to herself.

How was Allison following the command in Romans 12:10?

_____

_____

_____

_____

Allison felt she was obeying God's voice, but things hadn't turned out well. Should she give up on trying to reach out to Karen? Why or why not?

_____

_____

_____

_____

What *should* Allison do about the situation?

_____

_____

_____

_____

Allison decided to pray for Karen and asked God to help her with whatever she was dealing with in her life. She also prayed that God would help her not to be upset and not to feel that she had done something wrong.

On the following Monday, Karen found Allison at her locker. "Listen," she said. "I'm sorry I was such a jerk the other day. Changing schools has really stunk, and I guess I took it out on you. I'm really sorry. Friends?"

Boy, it would have been really easy for Karen to bail on God on Friday, but then she wouldn't have seen the great thing that happened on Monday! Even when it seems crazy to keep on trusting God, it's important to stand firm. Today, pray that you will always remember to rely on God and obey what you know He is telling you to do, no matter *what* happens.

TO OBEY OR NOT TO OBEY?

Obeying God's voice and doing what He asks often takes a great step of faith. In the Bible, we find that people often had as much trouble with this as we do today. Here are some examples of biblical characters who obeyed God's voice, of some who did not, and of what happened in each case.

Noah was a righteous man who lived in an *un*righteous society. The people's wickedness so offended God that He said to Noah, "I am going to put an end to all people" (Genesis 6:13). He told Noah to build an Ark made of cypress wood and to place him and his family and two of every kind of living creature, male and female, into it because He was going to send a flood. This must have seemed strange to Noah, but he "did everything just as God commanded him" (verse 22), and he and all those in the Ark were spared.

Moses had to step out in faith and follow God's voice time and again. After God called to him in the burning bush, He instructed Moses to go to Pharaoh, king of Egypt, and tell him to free God's people. The result? Pharaoh made it tougher on the Israelites and worked them harder (see Exodus 5). This had to be a setback, but Moses persevered and followed God. Ultimately, "He led them out of Egypt and did wonders and miraculous signs in Egypt, at the Red Sea and for forty years in the desert" (Acts 7:36).

Moses' brother, Aaron, had two sons named Nadab and Abihu. Nadab and Abibu were priests who had been given specific directions on how to handle sacrifices to the Lord. However, the brothers decided to disobey and do things their own way, and it immediately cost them their lives (see Leviticus 10:1-5).

Joshua followed in Moses' footsteps and obeyed God. At one point, God told him to have the Israelites march around the enemy city of Jericho for six days. On the seventh day, they were to march around it seven times, and then the priests were to blow trumpets. They did, the walls fell in, and the Israelites conquered the city (see Joshua 6). This victory was followed by a setback when a man named Achan disobeyed God's command not to take certain spoils from Jericho, and the Israelites were defeated in their next battle at Ai (see Joshua 7).

God often asked the Old Testament prophets to do things that seem strange to us. Ezekiel was told to eat a scroll and prophesy to Israel (see Ezekiel 3:1), construct a model of Jerusalem and lay siege to it (see 4:1-3), and lie on one side for 390 days (see 4:4-5). Hosea was told to name two of his kids "Not Loved" and "Not My People" (see Hosea 1:6-9). Jeremiah was asked to make a yoke and wear it when he prophesied (see Jeremiah 27). These prophets obeyed, but one who did not was Jonah. When God asked him to prophesy to Nineveh, he took a boat headed in the opposite direction. So God sent a storm, Jonah went overboard, a fish swallowed him, and he ended up back where he started (see Jonah 1–3). He eventually obeyed God's voice.

In the New Testament, Joseph was going to break off his engagement to Mary, but he obeyed God's voice and took her for his wife (see Matthew 1:18-24). Later, he heeded God's command to take Mary and Jesus to Egypt to escape King Herod (see 2:13-15). Peter, a bit unsteady at first as far as disciples go, ended up being the Rock that Jesus said he would be (see Matthew 16:18). At one point, when he and the other disciples were facing persecution, they declared, "We must obey God rather than men!" (Acts 5:29). Peter ended up becoming a great leader in the Early Church. The apostle Paul also heeded God's voice on the road to Damascus, God turned his life around, and he became instrumental in spreading the gospel to the Gentiles (see Acts 9).

So, what do we learn from these stories? From Noah and Joshua, we learn that we must obey God even when it might not make sense for us to do so. From Moses, we learn that obeying God doesn't always mean things will turn out well right away—but that God will bless us for our obedience in the long run. From Achan, we learn that disobedience can have consequences not only for ourselves but also for others. From Ezekiel, Jeremiah and Hosea, we learn that God can use our lives as lessons for others. From Jonah, we discover that it's always easier to just obey God's voice in the first place. From Joseph, we see that God has our best interests in mind when He asks us to do something. And from Peter and Paul, we see that when we follow God, He can use us to do great things in the world.

ENDNOTES

Session 1: Seeking God's Voice in His Word

1. The theme of divine presence so prominent in Joshua 1:1-9 has its roots in the nomadic lives of the Old Testament patriarchs, especially Isaac, Jacob and Joseph. At times, God's promise to be with His people was connected to a fearful journey (see Genesis 28:15; 31:3; Exodus 3:12) or as they entered into war (see Numbers 14:43; Judges 6:11-16; 1 Samuel 17:37). Thus, the theme of God "being with" His people to accompany, lead, protect and fight for them is a basic root of the Israelite faith.

Session 2: Seeking God's Voice for Guidance

1. Notice that after the Israelite leaders realize the deception, they develop a plan of action that is just as cunning as that of the Gibeonites—they reduce them to insignificant service. This must have come as a surprise to the Gibeonites, who were looking for military protection, not lifelong serivce. Thus, after Israelite leaders have sinned, they demonstrate wisdom and creativity in how they recover from the setback.

Session 3: Seeking God's Voice for His Vision

1. Note that while Joshua is "old and well advanced in years," God's words to him in Joshua 13:1-7 lack one crucial ingredient: who will take over for him when he steps down. In fact, leadership is not the issue here, because the Israelites will remain under the control of the same leader: God. Ultimately, His role as Shepherd overshadows the position of human leadership.
2. Dr. Martin Luther King, Jr. gave this 17-minute "I Have a Dream" speech on August 28, 1963, from the steps of the Lincoln Memorial in Washington, DC. The speech was part of the March on Washington for Jobs and Freedom and was a defining moment for the American Civil Rights Movement. After the speech and the march, *TIME* magazine named Dr. King "Man of the Year" for 1963. In 1964, he became the youngest person ever awarded the Nobel Peace Prize.

Session 4: Seeking God's Voice for Strength

1. Gallio's decision was profound, as if he had accepted the Jewish charge and found Paul guilty of a crime, he would have set a new precedent that would have handicapped Paul's efforts to spread the gospel. Gallio's refusal to act signified that Christianity was a valid religion throughout the Roman world, and for the decade of the AD 50s, the Christian message could be proclaimed without fear of violating Roman law.

Session 5: Seeking God's Voice for Transformation

1. This type of uncertainty is also reflected in Paul's appeal for prayer in Romans 15:30-32 that he would be delivered from danger in Jerusalem and that his gifts for the church there will be gratefully received.

Session 6: Seeking God's Voice in Sharing the Gospel

1. In many ways, the historical climate of Rome worked against Paul's message. The Jews had been expelled from Rome in AD 49 or 50 because of riots about Christianity (see Acts 18:2) and had only recently returned to the city after Emperor Claudius's death in AD 54. Thus, when Paul arrives in Rome in approximately AD 61, many people did not want to risk their position in the city or in their own religious circles to side with him and his Christian message.

Unit II: Obeying God's Voice

1. J. P. Moreland, *Love Your God with All Your Mind* (Colorado Springs, CO: NavPress Publishing, 1997), p. 15.

Session 7: Obeying God's Voice for Salvation

1. As Paul indicates in this passage, "faith" is more than just believing in God. Paul uses the word to mean our *accepting* what God has done in Christ rather than trying to earn our salvation by works. Our actions because of and on behalf of Christ are evidence of having been made alive with Christ. Ultimately, faith is our intimate attachment to Christ that produces our good works, proving that while we cannot earn savation, receiving it through Christ changes us.

Session 8: Obeying God's Voice for Power

1. According to Bible commentator William Lane, "The healing of the possessed boy demonstrates what faith expressed through prayer could have accomplished." (William L. Lane, *The New International Commentary on the New Testament:* Mark [Grand Rapids, MI: Eerdmans Publishing, 1974], pp. 329-332.) In Jesus' absence, the disciples stood in His place and had His authority. In faith, we need to refuse to set limits on God's power but instead pray for God to reveal it. By asking Jesus for faith, and by doing the things He has asked us to do, we can accomplish astounding things in His name (see Matthew 17:20).

Session 9: Obeying God's Voice and Doing Good

1. James's concern in this passage is to contrast true faith with dead faith, not faith with deeds. He provides three examples of "faith" in this passage: (1) faith without deeds, (2) the demons' faith, and (3) faith with deeds. For James, only the latter would be considered true faith—good deeds are a necessary and inseparable part of faith. True faith changes a person's heart and results in acts of compassion, specifically toward those who are less fortunate.

Session 10: Obeying God's Voice in Times of Waiting

1. Although the Bible makes no direct mention of Sarah's faith, the Lord's gentleness with her indicates that she was an equally important player in this story. The story in Genesis 18:9-15 actually concerns the Lord and Sarah—God had already appeared to Abraham and made the promise of the son, so there would be no need to repeat that promise to Abraham again. As a married woman, she demurely stays out of sight of the visitors, but God addresses her by talking to Abraham. Also, even though Sarah lied to cover up her disbelief, the Lord's response ("Yes, you did laugh") foreshadows her coming laughter at the birth of her son, whom she will actually name "he laughs" (Hebrew *Yitshak*, or "Isaac").
2. "World's Oldest Mother, 70, Lies Dying with Baby at Her Side After Risking Her Life to Beat Stigma of Being Barren," MailOnline, June 15, 2010. http://www.dailymail.co.uk/news/article-1286412/Worlds-oldest-mother-Rajo-Devi-Lohan-reveals-dying.html.

Session 11: Obeying God's Voice and Walking in Faith

1. In this story, as elsewhere in faith accounts, God's power and faith work in a cycle. God, through His power, creates an opportunity for the Israelites; and the Israelites, in turn, recognize God at work and take advantage of the opportunity. God, through His power, saves the Israelites from the Egyptians; and the Israelites, in turn, respond in awe and increase in their faith in Him. The Israelites could have refused salvation—just as we can choose today to refuse Christ—but they chose to act in faith, and that action in turn increased their faith.

Session 12: Obeying God's Voice at All Times

1. The first group of soldiers that God sent home were those who lacked the faith necessary to trust that the Lord could take care of them in the battle. If they had stayed, their lack of faith might have had a negative effect on Gideon's army and infected the rest of the soldiers. However, note that as the Midanites fled toward the Jordan River, Gideon sent messengers ahead to call out men to head them off. Those who responded were likely the men who had left—now encouraged by the turn of events, they were willing to fight. God doesn't want us to be on-again, off-again followers, but it is comforting to know that He offers grace when the faithless return to Him.

More *Uncommon* Junior High Resources for Leaders

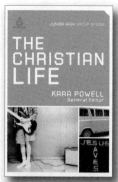

The Christian Life
ISBN 0-8307-4642-0
ISBN 978-0-8307-4642-2

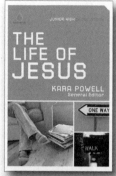

The Life of Jesus
ISBN 0-8307-4643-9
ISBN 978-0-8307-4343-9

Friends & Peer Pressure
ISBN 0-8307-4790-7
ISBN 978-0-8307-4790-0

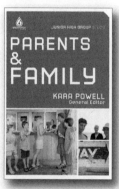

Parents & Family
ISBN 0-8307-5099-1
ISBN 978-0-8307-5099-3

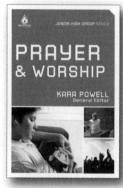

Prayer & Worship
ISBN 0-8307-5481-4
ISBN 978-0-8307-5481-6

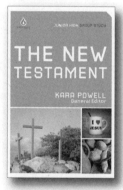

The New Testament
ISBN 0-8307-5522-5
ISBN 978-0-8307-5522-6

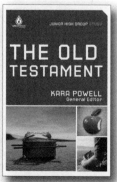

The Old Testament
ISBN 0-8307-5643-4
ISBN 978-0-8307-5643-8

Sharing Your Faith & Serving Others
ISBN 0-8307-5734-1
ISBN 978-0-8307-5734-3

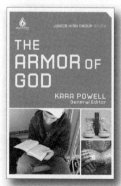

The Armor of God
ISBN 0-8307-5898-4
ISBN 978-0-8307-5898-2

Uncommon High School Resources for Leaders

The Christian Life
ISBN 0-8307-4644-7
ISBN 978-0-8307-4644-6

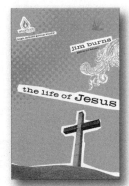

The Life of Jesus
ISBN 0-8307-4726-5
ISBN 978-0-8307-4726-9

Resisting Temptation
ISBN 0-8307-4789-3
ISBN 978-0-8307-4789-4

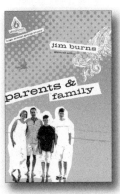

Parents & Family
ISBN 0-8307-5097-5
ISBN 978-0-8307-5097-9

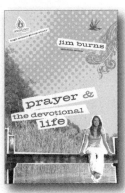

Prayer & Worship
ISBN 0-8307-5479-2
ISBN 978-0-8307-5479-3

The New Testament
ISBN 0-8307-5566-7
ISBN 978-0-8307-5566-0

The Old Testament
ISBN 0-8307-5645-0
ISBN 978-0-8307-5645-2

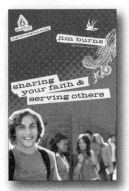

**Sharing Your Faith
& Serving Others**
ISBN 0-8307-5714-7
ISBN 978-0-8307-5714-5

Winning Spiritual Battles
ISBN 0-8307-5836-4
ISBN 978-0-8307-5836-4